The Fallen Few
of the Battle
# of Britain

For my father, Colin George McCrery, who served with the RAF for 30 years and was proud to be a member of an extraordinary band of brothers.

AND

For my father-in-law, Richard Copson who served with Bomber Command 1939-45 and never forgot his friends or experiences.

The Fallen Few
of the Battle
# of Britain

Nigel McCrery and Norman Franks

with Edward McManus

Pen & Sword
AVIATION

First published in Great Britain in 2015 by
Pen & Sword Aviation
An imprint of
Pen & Sword Books Ltd
47 Church Street
Barnsley
South Yorkshire
S70 2AS

ISBN 978 1 47382 787 5

A CIP catalogue entry for this book is available from the British Library.

Typeset in 10pt Dante by
Mac Style Ltd, Bridlington, East Yorkshire

Printed and bound in the UK by CPI Group (UK) Ltd, Croydon, CR0 4YY

Pen & Sword Books Ltd incorporates the imprints of Pen & Sword
Archaeology, Atlas, Aviation, Battleground, Discovery, Family History,
History, Maritime, Military, Naval, Politics, Railways, Select, Transport,
True Crime, and Fiction, Frontline Books, Leo Cooper, Praetorian Press,
Seaforth Publishing and Wharncliffe.

For a complete list of Pen & Sword titles please contact
PEN & SWORD BOOKS LIMITED
47 Church Street, Barnsley, South Yorkshire, S70 2AS, England
E-mail: enquiries@pen-and-sword.co.uk
Website: www.pen-and-sword.co.uk

Contents

Preface

Seventy-five years ago a comparative handful of mainly Royal Air Force fighter pilots was all that stood between Adolf Hitler's Luftwaffe and the British nation. Most of them were late teenagers or in early manhood; a small number had seen action in the first months of the Second World War, perhaps in Norway, over Belgium or in France. Those who had survived returned to add their somewhat limited experience to an aerial conflict which we now refer to as the Battle of Britain.

The total number of pilots who saw action between the official dates of 10 July and 31 October 1940 is recorded as 2,917. The majority came from the United Kingdom, but others came from New Zealand, Canada, Australia, Ireland, South Africa, Rhodesia, even the USA, while our near European neighbours, now allied to the cause of freedom, provided men from France, Belgium, Poland and Czechoslovakia. One came from Jamaica.

Many of these gallant young men did not survive the Battle; this number is recorded as 544. Of those who did survive, nearly another 800 did not live to see victory in 1945. This book concentrates on the 544 who were lost in this most important Battle, the first in history to be totally decided in the air. Some lasted longer than others, yet all contributed something to the victory that Fighter Command achieved in those perilous summer days of 1940.

The book contains a brief biography of those who fell in combat, and what befell them in those dangerous skies over southern England. Annually we remember all those fighter pilots who ran eagerly to their Spitfires or Hurricanes in order to defend our way of life – Churchill's 'Few'. One in five were killed. They should never be forgotten.

Nigel McCrery, Norman Franks and Edward McManus

The Few Who Died During the Battle

The basic acknowledgement that a pilot or member of aircrew flew operationally during the Battle of Britain was the rosette attached to their 1939-45 Star medal. To qualify he had to fly on at least one authorised operational sortie with an eligible squadron within Fighter Command, or those Coastal Command squadrons that were attached to Fighter Command, or fly as one of the Fleet Air Arm pilots seconded to the Command for operational duties. They totalled just over 2,900 men, who flew with seventy-one eligible squadrons.

All did their part, some, for many varied reasons, only briefly, others for long periods. There were many reasons for both. Death or wounding in battle ended the involvement of some, while a few others, operating near to a hostile coast, were brought down to become prisoners of war. Others quickly realised their talents should be used elsewhere. Those who survived their initial clashes with the German Air Force adapted quickly and with both luck, flying ability and eventually experience, continued to fight on during that summer of 1940, a number of them becoming what had become termed as aces. Many of course did survive the Battle, but over the next four years, were not so lucky and nearly 800 survivors fell in battles in other parts of the world, or died in training duties.

Those who died in the Battle numbered some 544, mostly in combat situations, but some in tragic training or test flights. As we reach the 75th Anniversary of this most iconic battle, the first battle to be fought entirely in the air, it is pertinent to record in a little more detail the lives of those who gave everything during that summer.

Most were regular members of the Royal Air Force, while others were from the Royal Air Force Volunteer Reserve, men who had given their free time to learn to fly, many acknowledging that a war with Germany was coming, and wanting to be ready. Within this group were men of the Auxiliary Air Force, who gave up weekends to fly with a number of County squadrons. When the Battle started it was obvious that many more pilots would be needed, if for no other reason than to fill the gaps caused by the inevitable casualties that would be sustained. The call for volunteer pilots went out to both Bomber Command and to the Royal Navy, and a number of pilots who had seen action as light bomber pilots during the Battle of France stepped forward, as did fifty-three pilots of the Navy's Fleet Air Arm.

In the meantime, men came from British colonies, Australia, New Zealand, Canada, South Africa and even a few American volunteers. Also arriving were men from countries in Europe already overtaken by the war, but who were determined to continue the fight. They wanted to see Germany defeated and to have their countries liberated from the new oppression of Hitler's Nazi Germany. Men from Poland, Czechoslovakia, France and Belgium arrived by many and varied circuitous routes.

Each did their part and their best. In 1961, Derek Wood and Derek Dempster had their book The Narrow Margin published by Hutchinson & Co Ltd. Twenty years had passed since the Battle and this was a wonderful study of the fight day by day. There had been other books, and more would follow, but for me (Norman Franks) it gave fresh input into the events of 1940. I was particularly impressed by their concluding words. I don't think they would mind if I quoted from their book. Wood, of course, died in 2003 at the age of 73, while Dempster died in 2012 aged 87.

> *The popular picture which has grown up in Britain around the Battle is not a true one. The picture is of a small band of invincible aces, brilliant, debonair and gay, flying into battle again and again, with vapour trails across the blue skies, shooting down German after German and occasionally falling themselves when outnumbered.*
>
> *Some squadrons were of course pre-eminent, usually because they were exceptionally well led. Because of their success they were kept longest in the forefront of the battle, and scored the greatest number of successes. In such squadrons as these there existed an élite who survived the longest and carried individually the heaviest burden of the Battle.*
>
> *Most of the squadrons were not like that, however. Many went into action confident and gay and withdrew as a battered remnant ten days or a fortnight later.*
>
> *There were they, very young and over-confident and inexperienced with little idea what it was all about. There were they, many thoroughly competent pilots, courageous and determined, but who lacked the speed and instinct needed to live long in action.*
>
> *But at the end of it they could nearly all claim that they had given a little better than they received.*
>
> *Scores of humble and unknown young pilots made up the squadrons. If they succeeded in scoring a victory or two before going down themselves, it was this that set the seal of victory on the preparations made before the war.*

What follows, therefore, is the list of those who did fall, and as can be seen, the majority did manage to inflict some hurt on their opponents, thereby blunting the German war machine, staving off a possible invasion, and keeping the British Empire safe.

At the time none would have imagined that seventy-five years later people would still be lauding their achievements and honouring those who did not survive, or wondering at what the fighter pilots achieved. They have indeed become as heroic emblems of British determination in the face of overwhelming adversity as the sailors who engaged the Spanish Armada, who formed the squares at Waterloo, who charged at Balaclava, or who defended Rourke's Drift. They would decry it all of course, for the men of the RAF had, since the days of WW1 modelled themselves as self-effacing, not wanting to 'shoot a line', to be modest. Despite that, they have made a name and a niche for themselves in our island history.

★ ★ ★

The official dates during which the Battle of Britain occurred are 10 July to 31 October 1940. While this is pretty arbitrary, and occasionally the start is noted as the first day of July, it has to be said that fighting had occurred before either of these July dates and after 31 October. However, we have chosen to go along with the official dates.

The Battle was later divided into separate phases. The first began on 10 July and lasted until 7 August. The Germans began by wanting to clear the English Channel of any hindrance to a possible invasion fleet, and while doing this they would be able to test Britain's defence strategy. Therefore this period was one of fighting over various small convoys still plying along the Channel. As the RAF had found during the Dunkirk evacuation, its pilots were not used to flying and fighting over water. Their tactics had been formulated around enemy bombers heading towards England from across the North Sea, out of their fighter escort range. Flying at the English or Scottish coasts it would not be too difficult to engage the raiders and simply line up for making passes at probably only small formations of bombers.

At Dunkirk the fighter pilots were out of their comfort zone, over miles of hostile sea, without dinghies (that didn't come into being in fighter aircraft until 1941) and often out of radio communication with their bases and controllers. Flight endurance was also a limiting factor, and while British radar techniques had improved tremendously it was still difficult to predict when attacking aircraft would begin an assault on shipping, so patrolling over convoys was time consuming and inevitably raiders would arrive just as it became necessary to head for home.

Nevertheless, actions were fought over these convoys from early July, or when raiders made a few attacks on places like Dover or Portsmouth, or the strange looking radar towers on the Isle of Wight.

So the First Phase started, and the first losses occurred.

July 1950

July 1940

Wednesday, 10 July 1940

The main attention of the Luftwaffe was a large convoy (in ballast), code-named Bread which had set off from the Thames Estuary at first light. It did not take long for enemy aircraft to start sniffing about and air battles took place during the day. Only one RAF fighter was lost in these actions with at least five others damaged. The Germans seemed to have lost nine of their aircraft with others flying home with various amounts of damage.

Early am   Sgt I C C Clenshaw RAFVR
                 253 Sqn
                 Hurricane P3359

Crashed in bad weather on a dawn patrol near Humber. Buried Kelvedon (St Mary) Churchyard extension, Essex. Aged 22. Joined the RAFVR in February 1939. He was officially the first pilot to die in the Battle.

10.00   F/O T P K Higgs RAF
              111 Sqn
              Hurricane P3671

Attacked by Oblt W Oesau, III/JG51 off Folkestone and collided with a Do17. Baled out but did not survive. Body washed up Dutch coast 15 August 1940. Buried Noordwijk General Cemetery. Aged 23 he was the son of Arthur H & Mrs Alice Higgs of Shepton Mallett, Somerset. At Merton College, Oxford he had achieved a BA Degree in Modern History. A member of the University Air Squadron he had joined the RAF in October 1938. The Dornier he collided with crashed near Dungeness.

Thursday, 11 July

Further enemy actions over the Channel during the day, many being reconnaissance aircraft. Three RAF fighters were lost with their pilots and two more from which pilots survived. More than a dozen hostiles were lost, including a He59 floatplane while on rescue duties. Three days later, the 14th, the British Government decided not to recognise these floatplanes even if showing a red cross, instructing RAF pilots to shoot them down. Some were shot down over the next weeks, and it must have been a worry for the fighter pilots, knowing that they might well contain fellow RAF pilots picked up from the sea.

08.00   Sgt F J P Dixon RAFVR
501 Sqn
Hurricane N2485

Shot down by Oblt L Fransisket, 7./JG27, south-east of Portland Bill. Baled out but drowned. Buried Abbeville Communal Cemetery, France. Aged 21, the son of Frederick A Dixon CMG DSO & Mrs Ethel H Dixon of Aldwick, Bognor Regis, Sussex. Had joined the RAFVR in late 1938, being posted to his squadron in France in June.

08.05   P/O G T M Mitchell AAF
609 Sqn
Spitfire L1095

Shot down by Oblt M Dobislav, 9./JG27 off Portland. Body washed ashore near Newport, IoW. Buried Willian (All Saints) Churchyard, Letchworth, Herts. Born in Ceylon he was 29, the son of Thomas R & Mrs Sarah A Mitchell of Letchworth, Hertfordshire. Member of the Cambridge University Air Squadron. In 1933 he was working in Sarawak, joining the AAF when back in England in November 1938.

08.10   F/L P H Barran RAF
609 Sqn
Spitfire L1069

Shot down by JG27 off Portland. Baled out wounded and burned and although rescued, died before reaching shore. Buried in his home town of Chapel Allerton, Leeds at the Lawns Wood Cemetery. Aged 31. Son of Philip A & Mrs Dorothy C Barron, of Chapel Allerton. Joined the Auxiliary Air Force in 1937.

Friday, 12 July
Another two convoys, one coded Booty, the other Agent held the German's attention

08.50   Sgt L Jowitt RAF
85 Sqn
Hurricane P2557

Brought down during attack on He111 of II/KG53 off Felixstowe. No known grave. Aged 28. From Thornton, Lancashire, son of Leonard & Mrs E J Jowitt. A former Halton Apprentice since 1928 – Fitter Airframes/Engines. Pre-war he saw service in the North-West Frontier, receiving the Mohmand Clasp to his General

Service Medal. Back in England he applied for pilot training gaining his 'wings' in 1938. Joining 85 he saw action in France.

Victories: 15 May   He111   Sh/Destroyed
           19 May   He111   Destroyed

09.45   F/O J H L Allen RAF
            151 Sqn
            Hurricane P3275

Hit by return fire from Do17 of II/KG2 off Orfordness. Crashed into the sea and lost. No known grave. From Remuera, Auckland, New Zealand, aged 25, the son of James H L & Mrs K P Allen (deceased), ward of Mrs Fanny M Edwards, of Napier, NZ. Both parents had died in the 1918 influenza pandemic, so brought up by his aunt. He came to England in 1933 to train as a seaman, winning the King's Gold Medal as a cadet with HMS Conway.

15.45   P/O D A Hewitt RAFVR
            501 Sqn
            Hurricane P3084

Brought down by return fire from a Do.17 off Portland. He has no known grave. Canadian, from Toronto. Aged 20, son of Dr Samuel R Hewitt MD & Mrs Edna D Hewitt. Joined the VR in early 1938, joining his Squadron in France in May 1940.

Victories: 27 May   sh/He111   Destroyed

Non-operational loss

?   Sgt S Ireland RAFVR
            610 Sqn
            Spitfire P9502

During dog-fight practice he lost control of his fighter during a dive and crashed at Titsey Park, Oxted, Surrey. He was 22 years old and his remains were taken back to his native Ireland, to be buried in Knockbreda Church of Ireland Cemetery, Newtownards, Belfast, Northern Ireland. He was the son of Robert & Mrs Sarah Ireland.

Saturday, 13 July

More sporadic attacks against convoys in the Channel, interception costing the RAF three pilots killed. Two enemy bombers and two fighters were known to have been shot down, with others damaged, by fighters and British AA fire.

11.36   Sgt P I Watson-Parker RAFVR
              610 Sqn
              Spitfire R6807

Crashed during patrol at Tatsfield, near Biggin Hill, Kent; cause not known. Buried in SS Peter & Paul Churchyard, Cudham, Kent. Aged 22.

15.20   F/L J C Kennedy RAF
              238 Sqn
              Hurricane P2950

Hit by return fire from Do17 of 2(F)123 over Chesil Beach. Possibly wounded he stalled and crashed at Southdown, Littlemore. Buried Warmwell (Holy Trinity) Churchyard, Dorset. Australian, from Sydney, aged 23. Son of John and Frances M Kennedy, of New South Wales. Joined the RAAF in 1936 then left Australia to join the RAF the next year, eventually joining 65 Squadron in December 1937. Posted to 238 as a flight commander at the end of May 1940.

16.45   Sgt J J Whitfield RAF
              56 Sqn
              Hurricane P2922

Shot down over the Channel by Oblt J Foezoe of 4./JG51. He has no known grave. From Goldthorpe, Yorkshire, aged 25. Son of Joseph & Emma Whitfield of Goldthorpe. Joined the RAF in November 1935 as an aircraft hand before selection as a pilot. Joined 56 in April 1940.

16.45   Sgt J R Cowsill RAFVR
              56 Sqn
              Hurricane N2432

Shot down over the Channel by Fw. H John of 4./JG51. He has no known grave. From Northumberland, aged 20. Son of Charles F R & Mrs Nellie Cowsill of Muncaster, Cumberland.

Victories: 13 Jul   Ju87   Damaged*
                (*This Ju87 crash landed at Cap Gris Nez.)

Non-operational loss

19.00   Sgt R R G Birch RAF
              19 Sqn
              Spitfire R6688

Crashed and burned at Bailsham, presumably stalled, while attempting a steep turn during dog-fight practice. He was 23, the son of Robert J & Mrs Caroline E Birch of St Pancras, London. Buried in Whittlesford (St Mary & St Andrew) Churchyard, near Duxford, Cambridgeshire.

Sunday, 14 July

Poor weather hampered operations and only one Hurricane was shot down by a German fighter. The Germans claimed five Hurricanes shot down north-east of Folkestone or south-east of Dover, four by JG51, one by JG3, all timed to agree with the time of the RAF loss.

15.30   P/O M R Mudie RAF
              615 Sqn
              Hurricane L1584

Shot down over Dover by Me109s of II/JG51, crashing into St Margaret's Bay. Baled out wounded, rescued by the Navy but died in Dover Hospital on the 15th. Buried Esher Cemetery, East Molesey, Surrey. Aged 24 he had joined the RAF in March 1939.

Monday, 15 July

No operational fatalities

Tuesday, 16 July

Non-operational loss

00.50   Sgt A D W Main RAFVR
              249 Sqn
              Hurricane P2995

Engine failed on take-off from RAF Leconfield, crashed and was killed. He was 22 and was cremated at Dundee Crematorium. His parents were Mr & Mrs D W Main of Dundee. Joined the VR in mid-1939 and posted to 249 on 28 May 1940.

Victories: 8 Jul   ½ Ju88   Destroyed

Wednesday, 17 July

?   F/O C D Peel AAF
               603 Sqn
               Spitfire K9916

Missing from operational sortie. From Haddington, East Lothian, aged 21. He has no known grave. He was the younger son of Lt-Colonel W E Peel DSO. Cheltenham College 1932-37. Joined his Squadron in 1938. Possibly the Spitfire claimed by Helmut Wick of 3./JG2, at 15.07 German time, south of the Isle of Wight.

Thursday, 18 July

10.00   P/O P Litchfield RAF
               610 Sqn
               Spitfire P9452

Shot down by Hptm H Tietzen of 6./JG51 north of Calais. Tietzen was killed in action on 18 August. Litchfield was 25 years old and has no known grave. Joined the VR in late 1937, and was commissioned to 610 Squadron in early 1940.

Victories: 27 May   Me110   Destroyed
              14 Jul   Me109   Damaged*
              (*the pilot of this 109 baled out near Boulogne)

10.00   P/O R L Patterson RAFVR
               Sgt R Y Tucker RAF
               Sgt L H M Reece RAFVR
               235 Sqn
               Blenheim N3541

Missing from operational patrol. Patterson came from Wormit, Fife, aged 26, son of John M & Mrs Helen S Patterson. Tucker came from Cumberland, aged 18, son of Anthony & Mrs Jane E Tucker of Leadgate, Cumberland. Reece was the observer, but no details of him are known. None of them have known graves. Probably shot down by Willi Melchert of 5./JG2.

12.15   P/O C R D Thomas RAF
             Sgt H D B Elsdon RAFVR (pictured bottom right)
             236 Sqn
             Blenheim L6779

Shot down by Major W Schellmann of Stab II./JG2 while engaged on a photographic mission over Le Havre. Thomas was buried in Quiberville Churchyard, France. He was aged 22, the son of Charles L & Mrs Constance M Thomas, and husband of Vera P Thomas of St Gennys, Cornwall. Elsdon, 28, came from from Southend-on-Sea, son of Mrs A B Elsdon. He has no known grave.

12.15   P/O R H Rigby RAF
             Sgt D D Mackinnon RAFVR
             236 Sqn
             Blenheim L6639

Photo recce to Le Havre. Shot down by Obfw W Schnell of II/JG2. Rigby (24) was buried in St Marie Cemetery, Le Havre, son of Howard and Mrs Ursula Rigby of Alsager, Stoke-on-Trent. Mackinnon (21), was the son of Duncan & Mrs Majorie G Mackinnon. Buried in Villerville Communal Cemetery, France.

Friday, 19 July

This morning saw the Boulton Paul Defiants take off from their airfield at West Malling. They had flown down from Turnhouse on 12 July. Shortly after 09.00 they flew down with twelve aircraft to their forward airfield at Hawkinge. At 12.23 they were ordered off to fly a patrol out to sea some twenty miles off the Kent coast, south of Folkestone. Three Defiants did not take off due to engine problems but the other nine headed out. Over the sea they were bounced by Me109s of JG54. The German fighter pilots, from the Stab flight and I and III Gruppen claimed twelve shot down, seven Defiants being lost. At this stage it was the worst single-squadron defeat during the Battle.

12.45   F/L I D G Donald RAF (left)
P/O A C Hamilton RAF (right)
141 Sqn
Defiant L7009

Shot down over Dover by JG51. Donald, son of Air Marshal Sir D G Donald DFC AFC, from Epsom, Surrey, was 25 years old and is buried in All Saints Churchyard, Tilford, Surrey. Hamilton, from North Harrow, Middlesex, was 28 and is buried in Folkestone New Cemetery, Kent. His parents were George A & Mrs Alice N M Hamilton.

12.45   P/O J R Kemp RAF (pictured)
Sgt R Crombie RAFVR
141 Sqn
Defiant L6974

Shot down by JG51 over Channel, off Dover. Kemp, from New Zealand, aged 25, has no known grave. His parents were Thomas S E & Mrs Ethel E C Kemp of Timaru, Canterbury, NZ. Crombie came from Lightwater, Surrey, aged 29, also has no known grave. He was the son of William & Mrs Mary Crombie, and husband of Mrs Phyllis E H Crombie of Lightwater.

12.45   P/O R A Howley RAF (pictured)
Sgt A G Curley RAFVR
141 Sqn
Defiant L6995

Shot down by JG51 off Dover. They have no known grave. Howley was 20 years old from Newfoundland; Curley, from Bushey, Hertfordshire, was 33. His parents were Major John and Mrs Jane A Curley of Bushey.

12.45   P/O R Kidson RAF (pictured)
Sgt F P J Atkins RAFVR
141 Sqn
Defiant L7015

Shot down off Dover by JG51. Kidson, from Wellington, New Zealand was 26, son of George R & Mrs Norah M Kidson. Atkins, also 26, was washed up on the French coast and is buried in Boulogne Eastern Cemetery. He was the son of Daniel and Eva Atkins of Oxford, and husband to Joyce E Atkins of Edmonton, Middlesex.

12.45   P/O J R Gardner RAF (safe) (pictured right)
P/O D M Slatter RAF (pictured left)
141 Sqn
Defiant L7016

Shot down off Dover by JG51. Gardner ditched, wounded, and was rescued, but Slatter did not get out and so has no known grave. Slatter came from Southsea, Hampshire, son of Wilfred T & Mrs Valletta M Slatter. He was 26 years old. Gardner was a New Zealander from Dunedin; he survived the war and retired with the rank of Group Captain in 1965 (RNZAF).

12.45   P/I I N MacDougall RAF (safe) (pictured)
Sgt J F Wise RAFVR
141 Sqn
Defiant L6983

Shot up by Me109s of JG51. Wise baled out over the sea and was missing. His pilot managed to get back to base unhurt. Wise was 20, and has no known grave. MacDougall survived the war with a DFC, awarded in 1942, retiring as an Air Commodore CBE. He died in 1987.

17.15   Sgt J A Buck
RAFVR
43 Sqn
Hurricane P3531

Shot down in combat by 9./JG27 off Selsey, probably by Fw. G Lehmann. Baled out over the sea but drowned. He was 24 and came from Manchester, the son of William A & Mrs Ellen Buck of Chorltonville, and husband to Mrs Rene Buck. He is buried in Stretford Cemetery, Lancashire.

Pictured from left to right: Sgt JA Buck, F/O PP Woods-Scawen, S/L CB Hull, S/L RL Wilkinson and Sgt GW Garton.

Saturday, 20 July

Another convoy action, this time above Bosom in Lyme Bay. In the early evening, RAF squadrons flying standing patrols, successfully engaged bombers and dive-bombers, plus fighters – eleven in all during the day. A number of enemy aircraft were shot down with others returning damaged to their airfields. It was the RAF's first significant victory in the Battle to date.

13.15   Sgt C Parkinson RAFVR
238 Sqn
Hurricane P3766

Shot down by Oblt G Homuth of 3./JG27 off Swanage. Baled out badly injured and rescued, but died the following day. He came from Coventry, aged 25, the son of George E & Mrs Mary H Parkinson of Coundon, Coventry. He was buried in St Michael's Churchyard, Stoke, Coventry.

Victories: 11 Jul   ½ Me110   Destroyed
13 Jul   ½ Do17   Destroyed

16.30   P/O E J H Sylvester DFC AAF
             501 Sqn
             Hurricane P3082

Shot down by Ltn I Zirkenbach of I./JG27 over the Channel, off Cherbourg. From Trowbridge, Wiltshire, he was 26 and has no known grave. Fought over France and at one stage was reported missing, but turned up safely. His DFC was not gazetted until April 1941, wef 27 June 1940. Educated at Harrow 1928-30 and commissioned into the AAF in January 1939.

Victories:	12 May	He111	Destroyed
	12 May	½Do17	Destroyed
	25 May	Do17	Damaged
	27 May	He111	Damaged

16.35   P/O F H Posener RAF
             152 Sqn
             Spitfire K9880

Shot down by Oblt G Homuth, 3./JG27 off Swanage. Missing. Aged 23, he came from South Africa, and has no known grave. Had joined the RAF on a short service commission in December 1938 and went to 152 Squadron in May 1940.

Pictured left to right: P/O Posener, P/O ES Hogg and P/O W Beaumont.

18.00   Sub-Lt G G R Bulmer RN
             32 Sqn
             Hurricane N2670

Shot down by Oblt. J Priller of 6./JG51 off Dover. Baled out but he drowned. He has no known grave and was 20 years old, the son of Leslie T & Mrs Mabel A Bulmer of Bradford, Yorkshire. He had joined the Fleet Air Arm in July 1939, and volunteered to fly with the RAF in 1940, joining 32 Squadron on 1 July.

18.00   F/O J F J Haworth RAF
             43 Sqn
             Hurricane P3964

Shot down into the Channel while investigating a He115 south of the Needles. Baled out but not rescued. He came from Teddington, Middx and was 23 years of age, the son of Captain and Mrs J Haworth. His body was not recovered so has no known grave. Joined the RAF in March 1937 and had been with 25 Squadron in 1938. Joined 43 on 11 June 1940.

18.20   Sgt E E Lockton RAFVR
               Sgt H Corcoran RAF
               236 Sqn
               Blenheim L1300

Shot down off Cherbourg during escort mission by Hptm. E Neumann of II./ JG27. Neither man has a known grave. Lockton came from Ashby-de-la-Zouche, Leicestershire, was 22, and son of Frederick W & Mrs Annie Lockton. Corcoran, 27, came from Higher Openshaw, Manchester. His parents were Edward and Mrs Lilly Corcoran.

Sunday, 21 July

A quiet day but there was still activity over the Channel. 7./JG27 claimed two Hurricanes, one being lost the other getting home damaged.

15.15   P/O R A De Mancha
               43 Sqn
               Hurricane P3973

Collided with a Me109 flown by Ltn H Kroker of 7./JG27, south of the Needles. He was 23 years of age and has no known grave. Kroker also died. Son of Ricardo A and Mrs Emma C De Mancha.

Victories: 13 Jul   sh/He111   Destroyed

Monday, 22 July

Non-operational loss

17.35   P/O J L Bickerdike
               85 Sqn
               Hurricane P3895

Killed in a flying accident near Castle Camps aerodrome, close to RAF Debden. Buried in Wimbush Parish Cemetery, Bristol. He was 23 years old and came from Christchurch, New Zealand.

Victories: 18 Jul   He111   Destroyed

Tuesday, 23 July

No operational fatalities

Wednesday, 24 July

?   P/O A M Cooper-Key
         46 Sqn
         Hurricane P2685

Killed during a forced landing near Peartree Station, Derby. Cause unknown. Buried Scopwick Church, Lincolnshire, aged 21.

12.30   F/O J L Allen DFC
         54 Sqn
         Spitfire R6710

Aircraft damaged in combat with Stab III/JG26 over Margate. Stalled while attempting to reach Manston and crashed near the Old Charles Inn, Cliftonville. Aged 24, he is buried in Margate Cemetery, Kent.

Victories:	21 May	Ju88	Probable
	23 May	Me109	Destroyed
	23 May	2Me109s	Probable
	24 May	Me109	Destroyed
	25 May	Me110	Destroyed
	25 May	Me110	Destroyed
	26 May	Me110	Destroyed
	26 May	Me110	Probable
	27 May	½Ju88	Destroyed
	17 June	Ju88	Destroyed
	9 Jul	He59	Destroyed
	9 Jul	Me109	Probable

12.50   P/O J R Hamar DFC
         151 Sqn
         Hurricane P3316

Crashed on North Weald aerodrome attempting an upward roll when he returned from a patrol. Dived inverted into the ground and was buried in Knighton Cemetery, Radnorshire, his home town. He was 25.

Victories:	17 May	Ju87	Probable
	22 May	Ju87	Destroyed
	22 May	Ju87	Probable
	25 May	Ju88	Destroyed
	29 May	Ju88	Destroyed
	9 Jul	Me109	Damaged
	14 Jul	Me109	Destroyed

It had not been a good day for 54 Squadron, especially with the loss of Johnnie Allen DFC. Pilot Officer H K F Matthews had been shot about but got home. The two German pilots who were responsible were Adolf Galland and Karl Straub of JG26. Two pilots of JG52 had claimed Spitfires at the same time and place. In the meantime, other 54 Squadron aircraft had returned with damage inflicted following attacks upon Dornier 17s, but whether 109s were involved is not clear.

Thursday, 25 July

14.55 F/O A J O Jeffrey DFC RAF
     64 Sqn
     Spitfire P9421

Shot down in combat over convoy off Dover. Body later recovered by the Germans and was buried in Vlissingen Northern Cemetery, Flushing in the Netherlands. He was 22 years of age and the son of John P & Mrs Elizabeth S Jeffrey of Edinburgh. His DFC was gazetted on 13 August. He had joined the RAF in 1937, and saw action over Dunkirk.

Victories:	1 Jun	Ju87	Destroyed
	7 Jul	Me110	Destroyed
	19 Jul	He115	Destroyed
	19 Jul	He115	Destroyed

15.00 F/L B H Way RAF
     54 Sqn
     Spitfire R6707

Shot down in combat with Me109s over convoy between Dover and Deal. From Hinton St George, Somerset, aged 22. Body later recovered and was buried in Oostdunkerke Communal Cemetery, Belgium. Son of Greville H & Mrs Dorothy C Way of Hinton St George, Somerset, Devon.

Victories:	13 Feb	½ He111	Destroyed
	25 May	Me110	Probable
	26 May	Me110	Probable
	3 Jul	½ Do17	Destroyed
	8 Jul	Me109	Destroyed
	8 Jul	½ Me109	Destroyed
	24 Jul	Me109	Probable
	24 Jul	Me109	Probable
	25 Jul	Me109	Destroyed

15.40 S/L A T Smith AAF

15

610 Sqn
Spitfire R6693

Crashed attempting to land at RAF Hawkinge after combat with Me109s over the Channel. From Liverpool, he is buried in St Peter's Churchyard, Delamere, Cheshire. He was 34 years old and married to Dorothy Smith of Manley, near Chester. His parents were Andrew T & Mrs Marie E G Smith. Smith was born in Liverpool in 1906 and went to Oundle School and Cambridge. Later a manager of a flour-milling company, he joined the AAF in 1936.

Victories:

27 May	Me110	Destroyed
27 May	Me110	Probable

17.45   Sub-Lt F Dawson-Paul FAA
64 Sqn
Spitfire L1035

Shot down off Channel during combat. Rescued by a German E-boat, severely wounded, and died on 30 July, being buried in Hardinghen Cemetery, France. From Chelsea, London, he was 24, son of Joseph D & Mrs Flavie L Paul.

Victories:

1 Jul	½ Do17	Destroyed
5 Jul	Me109	Destroyed
7 Jul	Me110	Destroyed
10 Jul	Me110	Destroyed
10 Jul	Me110	Destroyed
10 Jul	Me110	Probable
13 Jul	Me109	Destroyed
24 Jul	Do17	Destroyed
25 Jul	Me109	Destroyed

18.10   P/O A Finnie
RAFVR
54 Sqn
Spitfire R6816

Shot down by Me109s over Channel convoy off Dover. He crashed at Kingsdown and is buried in Margate Cemetery, Kent. He was 24. Joined the VR in late 1938, joining 54 on 8 July 1940.

23.45   P/O G K Gout RAF
234 Sqn
Spitfire P9493

Crashed near Porthowen, Cornwall, during routine night patrol. He was 24 years old and is buried in St Eval Churchyard, Cornwall. Son of Geoffrey D V & Mrs

Dorothy M Gout of Sevenoaks, Kent. Raced at Brooklands pre-war, joining the RAF in February 1939, going to 234 on 30 October.

Friday, 26 July

10.00   P/O P Chaloner Lindsey RAF
            601 Sqn
            Hurricane P2753

Shot down two miles off St Catherine's Point by Oblt. M Dobislav of 9./JG27. From Daresbury, Cheshire, his body was washed up on the French coast and buried in Wimereux Communal Cemetery. He was ten days past his 20th birthday. Son of Rev. Charles Chaloner Lindsey OBE & Mrs Mary Lindsey of Cheltenham, Glos. Joined the RAF in early 1938. On 17 August 1939 he was involved in a mid-air collision near Berwick-on-Tweed; realising one of his passengers did not have a parachute, Lindsey, despite a head injury and a broken leg, managed to get the aircraft down safely. He received a letter of appreciation from the Air Council for his courage.

Victories: 11 Jul   Me110   Destroyed

Saturday, 27 July

10.20   P/O J R Buchanan RAFVR
            609 Sqn
            Spitfire N3023

Shot down by Oblt. G Framm of 2./JG27 off Weymouth. He came from Iden, Kent but has no known grave. He was 25, the son of Bertram G & Mrs Kathleen A Buchanan. Joined the VR in late 1937. To 609 on 26 December 1939. His grave was restored 3/6/15. Name added to war memorial.

17.45   F/O P A N Cox RAF
            501 Sqn
            Hurricane P3808

Shot down by Fw. Fernsebner of 7./JG52 over Dover. From Brighton, he was 25, and has no known grave. An aircraft apprentice at Halton between 1932-35 (fitter) he won a place at Cranwell as a flight cadet in 1935. He was awarded the R M Groves Memorial Prize there, in 1937. Money was given by the family of the late Air Commodore Groves CBN DSO AFC Ld'h, DSM, who was killed in a flying accident in Egypt in May

1927, to reward cadets in flying navigation and research. With 43 Squadron in 1937 and then an instructor, he joined 501 in France in May 1940. Cox was the son of Dr. Arthur N Cox MD MRCP & Mrs Winifred A N Cox.

Victories:	20 Jul	Me109	Destroyed
	20 Jul	sh/Me109	Destroyed

Sunday, 28 July

14.20   P/O J H R Young RAF (standing, third from right)
74 Sqn
Spitfire P9547

Shot down by Hptm. A Galland of III/JG26 near the Goodwin Sands. He came from Boreham Wood, Hertfordshire, aged 22. He is buried in the Pihen-les-Guines Cemetery, France. Son of Captain James R & Mrs Augusta R Young of Dockenfield, Surrey. Joined the RAF in July 1939.

Monday, 29 July

07.45   F/O D R Gamblen RAF
41 Sqn
Spitfire N3038

Shot down in combat with JG51 near Dover during an action against Ju87s and Me109s. He was 25 years old and has no known grave. He joined the RAF in March 1937 and was with 41 Squadron by early July 1940.

07.45   F/Sgt C J Cooney RAF
56 Sqn
Hurricane P3879

Shot down by Me109 of JG51 off Dover. Crashed and blew up. From Rhos Robin, Denbighshire, son of John W & Mrs Emily Cooney, and husband to Charlotte Cooney. He has no known grave, and was 26 years old. He joined the RAF as an apprentice in January 1930, passing out as a metal rigger in late 1932. Applied for pilot training, ending up with 56 Squadron in early 1940, seeing action over Dunkirk.

Victories: 27 May   Me110   Probable

08.15   P/O K C Campbell RAFVR
43 Sqn
Hurricane L1955

Crashed following engine failure at Brabourne Lees, Kent. He was 28 and was buried in Lympne (St Stephen) Churchyard, Kent. He was the son of Kenneth C & Mrs Florence G Campbell of Pinner, Middlesex. Arrived on 43 Squadron in June 1940.

Tuesday, 30 July

No operational fatalities

Wednesday, 31 July

16.00   Sgt F W Eley RAFVR
74 Sqn
Spitfire P9398

Shot down off Folkestone Pier by Hptm. H Tietzen of 5./ JG51. He was 21 years old and is buried in St Margaret's Churchyard, Wrenbury cum Frith, Cheshire. There is a stained glass window in the Church in his honour. He had joined the RAFVR in 1939 and joined 74 Squadron on 15 February 1940.

16.00   P/O H R Gunn RAF (pictured top, third from left)
74 Sqn
Spitfire P9379

Shot down by Oblt. J Foezoe of 4./JG51. He was 27. His body was later recovered by the Germans and he is buried in Ostende New Communal Cemetery, Belgium. Son of Arthur G & Mrs Nellie P Gunn, husband to Vera G Gunn of Oxhey, Hertfordshire. RAF apprentice in August 1927, passing out as a fitter, aero-engines in 1932. After pilot training he was posted to 74 Squadron in early 1940.

August 1940

Thursday, 1 August

The Germans suffered a number of casualties on this day, but mainly due to British AA fire, or accidents. A couple more were written off after landing back home, their crews reporting damage from RAF fighters, although it isn't clear who had been involved. The luckless Henschel 126 shot down by Sub-lieutenant Kestin came from 4./(H)/31.

15.00   Sub-Lt I H Kestin RNVR
145 Sqn
Hurricane P3155

Hit by return fire while attacking a Hs126 believed to have come from 4(H)/31, over the Channel, south of Hastings and crashed into the sea. No known grave. Had been a flight instructor with the London Aero Club pre-war. Joining the FAA when war came he was initially with 758 Squadron; then volunteered to fly with Fighter Command. From Hatfield, Hertfordshire, he was the son of Herbert and Mrs Agnes Kestin, aged 23.

Victories: 1 Aug   Hs126   Destroyed

17.15   S/L P E Drew RAF
F/O B Nokes-Cooper RAFVR
236 Sqn
Blenheim N3601

Shot down during escort mission to Querqueville aerodrome, either by flak or by Oblt. W Adolph of III/JG27. Drew was the son of Air Commodore B C H Drew and Mrs Edith Drew of Seaview, Isle of Wight. He was 30 years old and was buried in Bivalle Churchyard, France. Nokes-Cooper was buried in Bayeux War Cemetery, France. He was the son of Joseph A and Mrs Georgina Nokes-Cooper, and husband to Phyllis, of Salford.

17.15   P/O B M McDonough RAF (pictured)
Sgt F A P Head RAFVR
236 Sqn
Blenheim R2774

Brought down either by ground fire or by Oblt. E Dullberg of 8./JG27 during escort sortie to Querqueville aerodrome. Crashed into the Channel so they have no known graves. McDonough came from Ulverston, Tasmania, the son of John and Nellie McDonough, and was nearing his 24th birthday. Head was 25 and had joined 236 in March 1940. On 11 July, flying with another pilot, they had a combat with a He111 over Start Point, Cornwall.

Friday, 2 August

Enough Polish pilots had arrived in Britain to help form No. 303 Polish Squadron at RAF Northolt, to join 302 Squadron that had formed on 17 July. There were a few clashes but overall a quiet day as regards air actions.

23.35   S/L H C Sawyer RAF
            65 Sqn
            Spitfire R6799

Crashed taking off for night patrol. He was 25 and was cremated at City of London Crematorium, East Ham. Cranwell cadet in January 1933, graduating the following year. His first posting was to 142 Squadron with Hawker Hart biplane bombers, which then saw service in the Middle East.

He was then appointed to the staff of the Electrical & Wireless School at Cranwell and later had a staff appointment there. Took command of 65 Squadron on 8 July.

Victories:	8 Jul	Me109	Destroyed
	24 Jul	Me109	Destroyed
	24 Jul	3 bombers	Damaged

Saturday, 3 August

No operational fatalities

Sunday, 4 August

No operational fatalities
Non-operational loss

?   Sgt J P Walsh RAFVR
            616 Sqn
            Spitfire N3271

During a dog-fight practice, his Spitfire went into a spin from 5,000 ft and did not recover before hitting the ground. Buried in Harrow Cemetery, Middlesex. Son of Harry P & Mrs Nellie Walsh of Harrow. He was 20.

Monday, 5 August

08.50   Sgt L R Isaac RAFVR
            64 Sqn
            Spitfire L1029

Shot down by R Seiler of 1./JG54 over the Channel. No known grave. He was 24 and came from Llanelly. His parents were James and Blodwen Isaac of Llanelly, Carmarthenshire.

Tuesday, 6 August

No operational fatalities

Non-operational loss

10.15   P/O H W A Britton RAF
17 Sqn
Hurricane N2456

Crashed and burned out at Debden Park shortly after take-off for a routine aeroplane air test. Actual cause not known. He was 19 years of age, son of Major Henry Britton, Royal Corps of Signals, and Mrs Olive M Britton of Edinburgh. Buried All Saints Churchyard, Wimbush, Essex.

Wednesday, 7 August

No operational fatalities

Thursday, 8 August

After the relative quiet of the previous few days, air actions on the 8th intensified, so much so that some historians chose this day as the start of the Battle of Britain. The main thrust was again against shipping in the Channel, with convoy C.W.9, code name Peewit being the target. This consisted of twenty ships that had sailed from the Medway the previous evening intent on passing Dover in the dark. However, German radar had picked it up and the dive-bomber crews were alerted. This day saw the largest concentration of enemy aircraft and the largest number of combats fought. The RAF claimed a large number of successes but they also suffered heavy losses in pilots killed, aircraft lost and pilots wounded or having to bale out. The Luftwaffe lost around ten Me109s and a Me110, plus seven Ju87 Stukas, with many others damaged. Yet another He59 was shot down in mid-Channel.

09.05   P/O L A Sears RAF
145 Sqn
Hurricane P2955

Shot down in combat by Unt. H Sippel of 1./JG27 south of the Isle of Wight. From Cambridge, he was 19, son of Charles H A and Mrs Maud E Sears. He has no known grave. He had joined the RAF in August 1939 and was sent to 145 in June 1940.

Victories: 1 Jul   sh/Do17   Destroyed

0915   Sgt E D Baker RAFVR
              145 Sqn
              Hurricane P3381

Shot down south of the Isle of Wight in a fight with I/JG27. He has no known grave. Son of Gerald D and Mrs Edith A Baker of Wimborne, Dorset, and husband to Evelyn. He was 28 years old and had joined the VR in January 1937. Once war came he was posted to 145 in October 1939.

11.40   Sgt D I Kirton RAF
              65 Sqn
              Spitfire K9911

Shot down in combat by Oblt. G Schöpfel of 9./JG26. He was 21, was born in Dover and is buried in St James' Cemetery, in his home town. Son of James H & Mrs Violet K Kirton of West Hampstead, London. Joined the RAF as a boy entrant in 1935, going to the RAF's School of Photography at Farnborough. Posted to 501 Squadron after training to be a pilot but quickly moved to 65 on 5 May 1940.

11.45   F/Sgt N T Phillips RAF
              65 Sqn
              Spitfire K9905

Shot down by Oblt. J Müncheberg of Stab./JG26 over Manston. He came from Gillingham, Kent, aged 31, and is buried in Chatham (Maidstone Road) Cemetery. Became an aircraft apprentice in 1924, passing out as a carpenter but his desire to fly eventually had him join 65 Squadron in early 1940.

Victories:	27 May	Do17	Destroyed
	7 Jul	Me109	Destroyed

11.55   F/O D N Grice RAFVR (pictured left)
              Sgt F J Keast AAF
              AC1 J B W Warren RAF
                 (pictured right)
              600 Sqn
              Blenheim L8665

Shot down by Oblt. G Schöpfel of 9./JG26 south of Ramsgate, although he claimed a Hampden. Grice, from Ealing, was 28 and cremated at the

Charing (Kent County) Crematorium. Married to Margaret, his parents were Neve J and Mrs Ethel A Grice. Keast, from Whitstable, Kent, 33, was the son of Arthur & Mrs Ann Keast of Swalecliffe, Kent. He is buried in Whitstable Cemetery. Warren, from Chelmsford, 19, was washed up and is buried in Calais Southern Cemetery, France. He was the son of Jeffery & Mrs Ethel Warren of Chelmsford, Essex.

12.00   F/L N M Hall AFC RAF
              257 Sqn
              Hurricane P2981

Shot down in combat with III/JG27 off St Catherine's Point, Isle of Wight. No known grave. From Hamble, Hampshire. His body was recovered and is buried in Criel-sur-Mer Communal Cemetery, France. He was 24, the son of Admiral S S Hall CB JP & Mrs Edith C Hall, of Kilcreggan, Dunbartonshire. He received his AFC in 1939 for work with meteorological flights while at RAF Mildenhall, Suffolk, after which he was with the Wireless Flight at RAE Farnborough.

12.00   Sgt K B Smith RAFVR
              257 Sqn
              Hurricane R4094

Shot down over the Channel off St Catherine's Point. No known grave. From Bromley, he was 21. His family lived in Grimsby, Herbert S & Mrs Ann D Smith. Joined the VR in August 1939 while working in insurance in London. Posted to 257 in May, his training cut short by the need to form new squadrons. Cruelly, after his loss, Lord Haw Haw, broadcast his name as being a prisoner of war, but he was not heard of again.

12.05   F/O B W J D'Arcy-Irvine RAFVR
              257 Sqn
              Hurricane P3058

Shot down in combat with III/JG27 off St Catherine's Point, Isle of Wight. He was 22 years old. Son of Henry C and Mrs C D'Arcy-Irvine, Serdang, Kedah, Malaya. Educated at Stowe and Cambridge, he became a member of the University Air Squadron in 1938 and then was commissioned into the RAFVR in October. He arrived on 257 on 14 May 1940. He has no known grave.

12.05   P/O P F Kennard-Davis RAF
            64 Sqn
            Spitfire L1039

Set on fire during combat with JG51 north of Dover, baling out while his aircraft crashed near West Langdon, Kent. Badly injured, he died two days later (10th). He was 19 years old and is buried in Brookwood Cemetery, Surrey. Son of Frank E & Mrs Frances A Kennard-Davis, of Selsey, Sussex. Had joined the Royal Navy at 16, but transferred to the RAF in May 1939. Arrived on 64 Squadron on 3 August, only to be shot down five days later.

12.45   F/L D E Turner RAFVR
            238 Sqn
            Hurricane P3823

Shot down in combat with Me109s over convoy Peewit south of Isle of Wight. No known grave. Born Port Stanley, Falkland Islands, he was 30 years of age. Working for Barclays Bank he was in the Artists Rifles as a territorial before going to the RAF in September 1932. His first three squadrons were 65, 74 and later 87, in 1937. Becoming a Reserve officer he came back when war started and posted to 238 on 13 July.

Victories:	20 Jul	Me109	Destroyed
	21 Jul	sh/Me110	Destroyed

12.50   F/O D C McCaw RAF
            238 Sqn
            Hurricane P3617

Shot down over convoy south of the Isle of Wight. Body recovered and was buried in Senneville-sur-Fécamp Churchyard, France. He was 24, the son of Captain Guy H McCaw MC (formally 3rd Hussars) and Mrs Renee M McCaw of Victoria, London. McCaw had been to King's College, Camridge and achieved a BA (Cantab). Joined the RAF in June 1938 as a direct entry, one of few places offered in competition each year to graduates in British and Commonwealth universities. Posted to 238 in May 1940.

Victories:	11 Jul	½ Me110	Destroyed

16.40   F/O Lord R U P Kay-Shuttleworth RAF
             145 Sqn
             Hurricane P3163

Missing in combat with Ju87s and Me110s over convoy south of the Isle of Wight. No known grave. He was 27 years old. Away from RAF service he was the 2nd Baron Shuttleworth of Gawthorpe, son of the late Captain the Hon. Lawrence U Kay-Shuttleworth RFA JP, and the Hon. Mrs Selina A Kay-Shuttleworth of South Kensington, London. His brother, Captain Edward Kay-Shuttleworth BA (Oxon), Royal Artillery, (3rd Baron) was killed in action in Tunisia, in November 1942 aged 25. Their father died in France as a Captain in the RFA, 30 March 1917, aged 29.

Victories:	11 Jul	sh/He111	Destroyed
	27 Jul	sh/Ju88	Destroyed

16.45   Sub-Lt F A Smith RN
             145 Sqn
             Hurricane P3545

Failed to return from combat south of the Isle of Wight. No known grave. He came from Barrow-in-Furness, then Stowmarket, and was 20 years old. Volunteered to fly with Fighter Command, joining 145 on 2 July 1940.

16.45   P/O J Cruttenden RAF
             43 Sqn
             Hurricane P3781

Shot down during combat ten miles south of the Isle of Wight, and crashed into the sea. No known grave. Aged 20, son of John & Mrs Elizabeth G Cruttenden. Joined the RAF in May 1938, and 43 on 9 June 1940.

16.45   P/O J R S Oelofse RAF
             43 Sqn
             Hurricane P3468

Shot down in combat south of the Isle of Wight. Body later recovered from the sea and buried in St Andrew's Churchyard, Tangmere, Sussex. Son of Johannes R and Mrs Hester S Oelofse of Johannesburg, South Africa. Joined the RAF in June 1939 and 43 on 8 February 1940.

23.48   P/O C F Cardnell RAFVR
Sgt C Stephens RAFVR
23 Sqn
Blenheim L1448

Crashed near Peterborough while on night patrol, cause unknown. Both killed. Carnell, 22, son of Charles F & Mrs Margaret Cardnell of Woodside Park, Middlesex, was buried in Highgate Cemetery, London. Stephens, 24, was buried St Crallo Churchyard, Coychurch Lower, Glamorganshire. He was the son of Thomas E & Mrs Ann Stephens of Bridgend.

Friday, 9 August

A quieter day but nevertheless a busy one for Luftwaffe crews, but only three of their aircraft were lost, one He111 to AA fire above the Humber, one to a Hurricane near Newcastle and one Ju88 over the Channel by five Hurricanes from 234 and 601 Squadrons.

16.45   Sgt R D Ritchie RAFVR
605 Sqn
Hurricane L2103

Possibly overcome by fumes during patrol off Dunbar, East Lothian, and crashed into the sea, suffering a broken neck. Body picked up by a ship. Is buried in Leslie Cemetery, Fife. He was 24, the son of Harry & Georgina J Ritchie of Leslie, Fife. Joined the VR in April 1939 and 605 in July 1940.

Saturday, 10 August

No operational fatalities

Sunday, 11 August

The Germans returned with massive air attacks and the RAF suffered accordingly. Thirty-one fighters were lost and only five pilots survived. The Germans suffered too, with over fifty aircraft lost or damaged, including two more He59s. These rescue aircraft were being better protected by this time, and 610 Squadron lost two pilots to escorting Me109s. However, a dozen Me109s failed to return to their bases during the day, plus ten Me110s. Four Stukas were also lost, plus three Ju88s and one He111.

10.30   F/O G R Branch EGM (GC) AAF
            145 Sqn
            Hurricane P2951

Shot down by fighters off Swanage. Body washed up on French coast and buried in Quiberville Churchyard, France. He was 26, son of Charles C Branch OBE & Mrs Mary M B Branch. Husband of Lady Prudence M Branch, daughter of the 6th Earl of Chichester. Won the EGM (later the George Medal) for saving the life of his pilot in a crash on 9 January 1938 by pulling him from the burning 'plane. The pilot was Aidan Crawley, later an MP and then Under-secretary of State for Air, and in 1955 editor of Independent TV. Educated at Eton and Bailliol College Oxford, Branch had joined the RAF in 1937 and been with 601 Squadron before 145.

Victories:	8 Aug	Ju87	Destroyed
	8 Aug	Ju87	Destroyed

10.35   F/O A Ostowicz KW
            145 Sqn
            Hurricane V7294

Shot down by fighters over Swanage and thought to have baled out. His aircraft appears to have crashed on the Isle of Wight. Polish, from Deblin born 22 May 1911, he has no known grave but may have been washed up on the French coast, where there is a grave to an unknown airman, next to F/O Guy Branch, in Quiberville Churchyard. He had arrived in England in late 1939, commissioned into the RAF in January 1940, moving to 145 on 16 July.

Victories:	19 Jul	½ He111	Destroyed

10.40   Sgt G Gledhill RAFVR
            238 Sqn
            Hurricane P2978

Shot down two miles east of Weymouth. Body washed up on French coast and buried in Criquebeuf-en-Caux Churchyard. Joined the VR in January 1939. Posted to 238 Squadron on 4 August, shot down one week later.

10.45   F/O S C Walch RAF
            238 Sqn
            Hurricane R4097

Shot down into Lyme Bay by Me109s. Born Tasmania, Australia, he has no known grave. Aged 23, the son of Percival B C and Mrs Florence H J Walch of Hobart. Joined the RAAF in July 1936, transferring to the RAF in August 1937. Once in

England he was trained and posted to 151 Squadron in January 1938. When war came he was sent as an acting flight commander to 238 on 12 May.

Victories:

11 Jul	Me110	Destroyed
20 Jul	½ Me109	Destroyed
21 Jul	Me110	Destroyed
26 Jul	Me109	Destroyed

10.48   F/O M J St borowski
238 Sqn
Hurricane P3819

Shot down by Me109 off Portland. Polish, aged 31, he has no known grave. Arrived in England in early 1940 and commissioned into the RAF, posted to 238 on 3 August..

Victories: 8 Aug   Me110   Destroyed

10.50   P/O F N Cawse RAFVR
238 Sqn
Hurricane P3222

Shot down by Me109 off Portland. Body washed up on French coast and buried in Cayeux-sur-Mer Communal Cemetery. He was 25 and son of Ernest F & Mrs Emma M Cawse of Bridgewater, Somerset. Joined the Squadron on 7 July.

10.45   P/O J L Smithers AAF
601 Sqn
Hurricane P3885

Shot down in combat over Portland. From Knockhalt, Kent. Body was recovered and buried in Sainte Marie Cemetery, Le Havre, France. He was 24 years old, son of Langley and Mrs Mabel L Smithers of South Kensington. His brother 2/Lt Alfred J L Smithers was killed in action with the 11th Hussars in North Africa in November 1941, aged 20.

10.50   F/O R S Demetriadi AAF
601 Sqn
Hurricane R4092

Shot down into the sea off Portland. Son of Sir Stephen & Lady Demetriadi KBE, of Westminster, Sussex and Manchester, attached to the King's Estate at Sandringham. His body was washed up on French coast and buried in Cayeux-sur-Mer Communal Cemetery. He was 21. His brother-in-law was Flying Officer W H Rhodes-Moorhouse DFC, who would be killed with 601 Squadron on 6 September.

10.50   F/O J Gillan RAF
601 Sqn
Hurricane P3783

Shot down off Portland. He was 26 years old and has no known grave. He had been with the Squadron eight days. Son of William M & Mrs Mary T Gillan of Aberdeen. Gillan joined the RAF in 1936, trained in Egypt and was then posted to 55 Squadron in Iraq. Returned to England in 1938 and after a period of instructing, he joined 601 on 3 August.

10.55   P/O W G Dickie RAFVR
601 Sqn
Hurricane L2057

Shot down off Portland. No known grave. From Dundee, Scotland, aged 24, son of William B & Mrs Euphemia Dickie. Joined the VR in early 1939, posted to 601 on 8 June.

Victories: 7 Jul   sh/Do17   Destroyed

10.50   F/L R V Jeff DFC & Bar, CdG RAF
87 Sqn
Hurricane V7231

Failed to return when chasing enemy aircraft off Portland Bill. No known grave. From Tenby, Pembrokeshire, he was born in Kuala Lumpur, Malay States. Aged 27, son of Ernest & Mrs Madge Jeff. Joined the RAF in October 1936, by the summer of 1937 was with 87 Squadron, and went to France with them when war began. His DFC was among the earliest awarded (March 1940) and the Bar came in June. He is also referred to sometimes as Voase Jeff.

Victories:

2 Nov '39	He111	Destroyed
10 May	Do17	Destroyed
15 May	Do17	Destroyed
20 May	Me109	Destroyed

Plus one unknown EA destroyed

11.00 P/O J S B Jones RAF
152 Sqn
Spitfire R6614

Shot down over Channel by Me109. Jones seen to bale out but did not survive. Body recovered and buried in Sainte Marie Cemetery, Le Havre, France. He was 21 years old, from Marlborough, Wiltshire, son of Group Captain J H O Jones, who was CO of RAF Oban, Scotland, and who had been CO of Cranwell in 1936.

Victories:

27 Feb	½ He111	Destroyed
25 Jul	Me109	Destroyed

11.00 F/L R D G Wight DFC RAF
213 Sqn
Hurricane N2650

Missing after combat over Portland. From Skelmorlie, Ayrshire, he was 24. Body recovered and buried in Cayeux-sur-Mer Cemetery, France. Son of John E & Mrs Ethel Wight of Hale, Cheshire. Commissioned into the RAF in 1934, served with 208 Squadron in Egypt, later with 29 Squadron and then 64. Returning to England he had flown with 72 Squadron before moving to 213 in February 1939 as a flight commander. Flew in France in May 1940. His DFC was gazetted in June 1940.

Victories:

19 May	Me109	Probable
19 May	sh/Hs126	Destroyed
20 May	½ Do17	Probable
20 May	Me110	Probable
20 May	sh/Hs126	Destroyed
27 May	Me109	Destroyed
27 May	Me109	Destroyed
28 May	Me109	Destroyed
28 May	Me109	Probable
28 May	Me109	Probable

28 May	He111	Probable
30 May	Do17	Probable
31 May	Me109	Destroyed
31 May	Me109	Destroyed

11.00 Sgt S L Butterfield DFM RAF
213 Sqn
Hurricane P3789

Shot down by fighters off Portland Bill. His body was later recovered and buried in Boulogne Eastern Cemetery, France. He was 27, from Leeds, son of Samuel H & Mrs Evelyn Butterfield, and husband to Dorothy L Butterfield of Windsor. A former aircraft apprentice (metal rigger) in 1932 he volunteered to become a pilot and was with 213 by early 1940.

Victories:	19 May	½ Hs126	Destroyed
	20 May	¼ Hs126	Destroyed
	28 May	Me109	Destroyed
	28 May	Me109	Destroyed
	28 May	Ju88	Destroyed
	28 May	Me110	Destroyed
	31 May	Me109	Destroyed
	31 May	Me109	Probable

11.20 P/O J A J Davey RAF
1 Sqn
Hurricane P3172

Hit by fire from Me110, crashed on Sandown Golf Course while trying to force land. From Leamington Spa, Warwickshire, he was 20, and is buried in nearby Sandown Cemetery, Isle of Wight. Son of Arthur H & Mrs Elsie M Davey of Leamington Spa. RAF Cadetship. Joined the Squadron on 15 July.

11.30 F/Sgt J H Tanner RAF
610 Sqn
Spitfire R6918

Failed to return from patrol over the Channel. Body recovered and buried in Calais Southern Cemetery. Aged 25, son of John W & Mrs Ever E Tanner of Enfield, Middlesex, husband of Helen M Tanner. Became an aircraft apprentice in 1931 (fitter), later applying for pilot training. By early 1940 he was with 610 Squadron.

11.30   Sgt W J Neville RAFVR
610 Sqn
Spitfire R6630

Missing from patrol over the Channel. No known grave. Came from Shepperton, Middlesex, he was 26 years old. Son of William J & Mrs Julia K Neville of Shepperton, Middlesex. Joined the Squadron on 27 July.

12.15   P/O D G Cobden RAF
74 Sqn
Spitfire R6757

Lost in combat with Me110s thirty miles east of Harwich on his 26th birthday. Body recovered and buried in Ostende New Communal Cemetery, Belgium. Had previously had brief postings to 3 and 615 Squadrons. He came from Christchurch, New Zealand, son of Alfred P & Mrs Mabel E Cobden of Papanui, Canterbury, NZ.

Victories:	24 May	sh/Do17	Destroyed
	26 May	sh/Hs126	Probable
	27 May	Do17	Probable
	10 July	Me109	Probable
	10 July	Do17	Damaged

12.15   P/O D N E Smith RAFVR
74 Sqn
Spitfire R6962

Shot down east of Harwich during combat over convoy. Body recovered and buried in Ostende New Communal Cemetery, Belgium. Joined the RAF in 1940 having been a transport pilot in the Spanish Republican Air Force in 1937. He was 24 by this time and joined 74 Squadron on 20 July, having at first been sent to No.24 Communication Squadron at RAF Hendon.

13.00   Sgt R D Baker RAF
56 Sqn
Hurricane N2667

Believed to have been shot down by lone Spitfire during a convoy patrol. Baled out into the sea but was picked up dead. Buried in Letchworth Cemetery, Hertfordshire. He was 23, son of David & Florence A Baker, and husband of Olive R

Baker of Rainham, Kent. Joined the RAF in 1934 as an aircraft hand. Training to be a pilot he was posted to 56 Squadron in early 1940.

Victories: | | | |
|---|---|---|
| 27 May | He111 | Damaged |
| 29 May | He111 | Damaged |
| 13 July | Ju87 | Destroyed |

14.20   P/O J H H Copeman RAF (pictured middle)
111 Sqn
Hurricane P3105

Shot down off Margate by enemy fighters. Body recovered and buried in Middlekerke Communal Cemetery, Belgium. He was aged 27, son of George M & Mrs Blanche Copeman. Joined the RAF in August 1938 and by the time war began was with 111 Squadron.

Victories: | | | |
|---|---|---|
| 17 Jul | Me109 | Damaged |
| 31 Jul | Ju88 | Destroyed |

14.20   P/O J W McKenzie RAF
111 Sqn
Hurricane P3922

Shot down by Me109 off Margate. From Johannesburg, aged 20, he has no known grave. Son of Archibald & Mabel McKenzie of Jo'burg, Transvaal. Had entered the RAF College Cranwell in January 1938, flying with 263 Squadron shortly after war was declared. Had seen service in Norway during April 1940, having flown off the carrier HMS Glorious. Sent to 111 on 10 May.

14.20   Sgt R B Sim RAFVR
111 Sqn
Hurricane P3942

Lost during combat with Me109s over Margate. From Kilmarnock, North Ayreshire, he was 23 and has no known grave. Son of William W & Mrs Annie Sim of Stewarton, Ayrshire. Joined the VR in 1938. Went to 111 Squadron on 6 July.

14.25   P/O R R Wilson RAFVR
111 Sqn
Hurricane P3595

Shot down in combat with Me109s over Margate. No known grave. From Moncton, New Brunswick, Canada, he was aged 20. Son of Roy H & Mrs Ivy K Wilson. Commissioned into the RAF in October 1938, joining 111 Squadron on 23 May 1940.

Victories:	2 Jun	Me109	Destroyed
	2 Jun	Me109	Damaged
	25 Jul	Me109	Destroyed

Monday, 12 August

Today was just as bad, as the Germans tried to knock out British radar stations around the coast. Convoys were also targets, Agent and Arena off the North Foreland. The Germans had also started to fly cover for returning bombers, making it dangerous to chase aircraft across towards France. Twenty RAF fighters were lost and only two pilots survived shoot downs. Ju88 formations were badly mauled, nine being brought down, plus five Me110s and eleven Me109s.

11.00   P/O R W G Beley RAF
              151 Sqn
              Hurricane P3304

Shot down in combat with Me109s off Ramsgate. Rescued but died of his wounds at Manston. Canadian, aged 20 from British Columbia. Buried in Margate Cemetery. Commissioned into the RAF in March 1940, and posted to 151 on 14 July.

12.20   F/L L C Withall RAF
              152 Sqn
              Spitfire P9456

Missing after combat with Me109s south of Isle of Wight. From Canberra, Australia, aged 29. No known grave. Son of Latham and Mrs Mabel Withall of Ealing, Middlesex. Joined the RAF in October 1936 and went to 152 in October 1939 as a flight commander.

12.20   P/O D C Shepley RAF
              152 Sqn
              Spitfire K9999

Shot down by fighters south of the Isle of Wight. Born Carlton-in-Lindrick, Nottinghamshire. He has no known grave and was 22 years old. Son of J T & Mrs Lillie E Shepley of Holmesfield, Derbyshire, and husband of Mrs F E Shepley. Oundle School 1932-35. Entered RAF College at Cranwell in January 1938, and upon graduation was sent to 152 in September 1939.

Victories: 8 Aug   Me109   Destroyed
               11 Aug   Me109   Destroyed

12.30   P/O J H Harrison RAFVR
              145 Sqn
              Hurricane R4180

Shot down during combat with Me110s and Ju88s south of the Isle of Wight. From Mitcham, Surrey, he was 22. No known grave. Son of Dr Arthur W Harrison MD and Mrs Lilian J Harrison. After a period with the Territorial Army he joined the RAFVR in 1937 and after training went to 145 Squadron on 31 July 1940.

12.30   F/Sgt J Kwieciński
               145 Sqn
               Hurricane P3391

Lost during combat south of the Isle of Wight. Aged 23, he has no known grave. Polish pilot who arrived in England in February 1940. There is a suggestion that he was briefly with 601 Squadron, but joined 145 on 4 August.

12.30   F/L W Pankratz
               145 Sqn
               Hurricane R4176

Missing after combat south of the Isle of Wight. Polish, aged 26, he has no known grave. Polish Air Force pre-war and commissioned into the RAF in January 1940. Posted to 145 on 16 July.

12.35   P/O D G Ashton RAFVR
               266 Sqn
               Spitfire P9333

Shot down in flames off Portsmouth. Body later recovered in September by a minesweeper and buried at sea. Aged 20, he came from Keyworth, Nottinghamshire, the son of Richard T C & Mrs Evelyn M Ashton. Joined the VR in June 1938 and was with 266 as the Battle started.

12.44   Sgt G N Wilkes RAFVR
               213 Sqn
               Hurricane P2802

Missing after action off Bognor. From Horley, Surrey, he was 21 and has no known grave. Son of Sidney A & Mrs Georgina E S Wilkes of Horley. Joined the VR in February 1938, posted to 213 on 8 June 1940.

12.45   Sgt S G Stuckey RAF
               213 Sqn
               Hurricane P2802

Lost after combat off Bognor. From Bristol, he has no known grave and was 26. Son of Sidney J and Mrs Anne F Stuckey of Bristol. Joined the RAF in May 1936 as an aircraft hand but applied for pilot training and by the summer of 1939 was with 73 Squadron, going with it to France. Once back in England he was posted to 213 in June 1940.

12.55   F/O K Łukaszewicz
               501 Sqn
               Hurricane P3803

Shot down west of Ramsgate during combat with fighters. Polish, aged 27. He had been in the Polish Air Force pre-war and made his way to England, arriving in January 1940. Joined 302 Squadron on 26 July, then moved to 501 on 7 August.

13.00   P/O J A G Chomley RAF
               257 Sqn
               Hurricane P3662

Failed to return from an action off Portsmouth. From Southern Rhodesia, he was 20 years old. No known grave. Son of Major George G & Mrs Nancy Chomley of Bolton, Marandellas, Southern Rhodesia. Joined the RAF around January 1940 and posted to 257 on 7 July.

Tuesday, 13 August Adler Tag

'Eagle Day' the Germans named it, the day they began Adlerangriff (to destroy the RAF) in preparation to mount their invasion of England. This was termed the Second Phase of the Battle. It should have started on the 12th, but poor weather delayed it until the 13th. It began with raids on coastal airfields and forward landing grounds, and these would gradually progress inland in the following weeks, and included more attacks on British radar sites.

The Channel battles had proved a valuable testing period but now the main event was underway. First, however, the Luftwaffe needed to clear the sky of RAF fighters and be able to maintain air superiority over both the Channel and the proposed landing areas along the south coast of England. The day would cost the RAF around 13 fighters, while the Germans suffered 47 lost and 39 more damaged.

08.00   F/O R L Glyde DFC RAF
               87 Sqn
               Hurricane P3387

Hit by return fire from a Ju88 off Selsey Bill. From Perth, Australia, aged 26. No known grave. Son of Frank C & Mrs Phillis N Glyde of Claremont, Western Australia. Joined the RAAF in 1935 but had to leave following the discovery of a medical condition. Getting over this he came to England and took a commission into the RAF in June 1937. He was with No.1 Anti Air Cooperation Unit at Farnborough, before being

posted to 87 Squadron in October 1938. Went to France with this unit when war began. He was interned in Belgium following a crash-landing on 14 November 1939 but 'allowed' to escape back to France two weeks later.

Victories:	19 May	¼ Hs126	Destroyed
	19 May	Me109	Probable
	19 May	Me109	Destroyed
	11 Jul	Me110	Damaged
	11 Jul	Me110	Destroyed
	13 Aug	sh/Ju88	Destroyed
	13 Aug	sh/He111	Destroyed

16.30   Sgt H J Marsh RAF
238 Sqn
Hurricane P3177

Missing in action with fighters over Portland. He was 27 and came from Merton Park, Surrey. No known grave. Son of Captain H Marsh RASC & Mrs Agnes Marsh. He had joined the RAF as a Halton apprentice in 1931, passing out as a fitter. Re-mustered as an airman observer in early 1939, he then applied for pilot training. Once completed he was sent to 253 Squadron in November 1939, then to 238 in July 1940.

Victories:	11 Aug	He111	Destroyed
	13 Aug	Me110	Destroyed

16.50   Sgt P P Norris RAFVR
213 Sqn
Hurricane P3348

Missing after combat over Portland. Born Burgess Hill, Sussex. Body washed ashore on French coast and buried in Étaples Military Cemetery. He was 22, son of William & Florence B Norris of Burgess Hill, Sussex. Joining the VR in the autumn of 1937 he was eventually posted to 213 Squadron on 9 March 1940.

Non-operational loss

19.15	P/O F S Gregory RAF
	65 Sqn
	Spitfire R6766

Crashed at Eastry while engaged on night flying practice, cause not known. He baled out too low and was killed. He was 21, the son of Richard T & Mrs Kathleen M Gregory of Potters Bar, Hertfordshire. Cremated in Enfield Crematorium. He had joined the VR in July 1938 and after training was sent to 65 Squadron on 6 July 1940.

Wednesday, 14 August

12.45	F/O P Collard DFC RAF
	615 Sqn
	Hurricane P3109

Failed to return from combat off Dover. Born in London, he was 24. His body was recovered and buried in Oye-Plage Communal Cemetery, France. Son of Charles J & Mrs Gladys M Collard, and husband of Mrs Annette C Collard of Ashtead, Surrey. Initially with the AAF before the war but still with 615. Went to France with this unit in November 1939 still with Gloster Gladiators until they began receiving Hurricanes in April 1940.

Victories:	15 May	Hs126	Damaged
	15 May	u/i EA	Damaged
	22 Jun	He111	Probable
	14 Jul	Ju87	Destroyed
	27 Jul	sh/He59	Destroyed

12.50	P/O C R Montgomery RAF
	615 Sqn
	Hurricane P3160

Shot down off Dover. Aged 26, his body was recovered and buried in Oye-Plage Communal Cemetery, France. Son of John & Mrs Mary E Montgomery of Fivemiletown, Co Tyrone, Northern Ireland. Joined the RAF in June 1939 and was posted to 615 in France on 14 May 1940.

17.30   F/O H MacD Goodwin AAF
609 Sqn
Spitfire N3024

Missing from operations over the south coast. Body washed up on the Isle of Wight ten days later and buried in St Cassian's Churchyard, Corbett, Worcs. From Hagley, Worcs., aged 25. His younger brother Barrie (23) had died in a flying accident on 24 June 1940 with 605 Squadron. They are buried next to each other. Sons of Laughton & Mrs Jessie Goodwin, Hagley, Hereford & Worcestershire. Commissioned into the Auxiliary Air Force in April 1933, he later became an RAFO officer, but relinquished this and returned to the Auxiliaries. On completion of his training went to 609 on 20 May 1940.

Victories:	12 Aug	Me110	Destroyed
	13 Aug	Ju87	Destroyed
	13 Aug	Ju87	Destroyed

19.15   Sgt H F Montgomery RAFVR
43 Sqn
Hurricane L1739

Failed to return from intercepting He111 forty miles south of Beachy Head. Body recovered and buried in Senneville-sur-Fécomp Churchyard, France. Joined the VR in February 1938, completed his training after the war began, and sent to 43 Squadron on 3 August 1940.

Thursday, 15 August

Today, two days after the start of the Luftwaffe's Adlerangriff, the Germans tried again to impose themselves against Fighter Command, but the weather was against them during the morning. Some reconnaissance missions were flown but it was after mid-day that the weather cleared sufficiently to begin operations. As it turned out it was to be the bitterest day's fighting both sides had seen and would be known as 'Black Thursday' by the German Air Force. Both sides suffered heavy casualties, but many RAF pilots were able to bale out safely, while others were wounded but alive. Some 27 fighters were lost but the Germans lost over 70, with others landing back home in damaged condition.

12.05   Sgt D W Halton RAFVR
                  615 Sqn
                  Hurricane P2801

Shot down by Me109, falling at Seal, near Sevenoaks. He has no known grave. He had joined the VR pre-war and was called up for service when war began. Completing his training he was posted to 615 in early July 1940.

15.00   P/O D O M Browne RAF
                  1 Sqn
                  Hurricane R4075

Missing after action with Me109s off Harwich. From Willesden, Middx, his family moved to Hove, Sussex, and joined the VR in December 1937. He was posted to 74 Squadron in April 1939, and later was with No.1 AACU at Farnborough. He was then sent to 1 Squadron in France on 21 May 1940. He helped damage a He111 on 19 June over the South Downs that was later shot down by 145 Squadron. He has no known grave. Son of Thomas M & Mrs Elsic L Browne of Portslade-by-Sea, Sussex. CWGC records his death as on the 16th.

Victories: 19 Jul   He111   Damaged*
                     (*finished off by Hurricanes of No.43 Sqn)

15.00   Sgt M M Shanahan RAFVR
                  1 Sqn
                  Hurricane P3043

Missing after action with Me109s off Harwich. From Seven Kings, Essex. He was 25 and has no known grave. Son of William & Mrs Catherine Shanahan, of Seven Kings, Essex. Joined the VR in January 1938 and eventually arrived on 1 Squadron on 3 August 1940.

15.20   F/O C J D Andreae RAFVR
                  66 Sqn
                  Spitfire R6990

Missing after fighter combat over the Channel. From London, he was 23 years old, went to Caius College, Cambridge, and was with their University Air Squadron. Commissioned into the RAFO in 1937 he then went into the RAFVR in early 1938. On 20 July 1940 he was posted to 64 Squadron. He has no known grave. Son of Frank G & Mrs Georgina Andreae of Paddington, London.

17.15   Sgt F B Hawley RAFVR
              266 Sqn
              Spitfire N3189

Missing after action against a He115 off Dunkirk. From Coventry he had joined the VR in May 1939 and completing his training was sent to 266 Squadron on 10 June 1940. Son of Frederick Thomas & Mrs Catherine E Hawley of Coventry. He has no known grave.

17.45   P/O M S H C Buchin RAFVR
              213 Sqn
              Hurricane V7227

Missing from air action over Portland. A former instructor with the Belgian Air Force this 34-year-old pilot escaped to France where he ferried aircraft for the French before getting away again, this time to England. He was commissioned into the RAFVR and sent to 213 Squadron on 23 July. He has no known grave but is named on the memorial at the Pelouse d'Honneur Cemetery at Brussels-Evere.

Victories: 11 Aug   Ju88   Destroyed

17.51   F/O B M Fisher RAFVR
              111 Sqn
              Hurricane P3944

Shot down in flames over Selsey while in combat with Ju88s and Me109s. Baled out but killed. He is buried in St John's Church Cemetery, Eton. He was educated at Eton and Trinity College Cambridge and commissioned into the RAFVR in July 1938; after becoming a pilot, was posted to 111 Squadron on 12 May 1940. Son of George and Janet Fisher. His older brother was F/O A G A Fisher who had also been in 111 for a while; later he became Sir Antony Fisher AFC.

18.00   S/L T G Lovell-Gregg RAF
              87 Sqn
              Hurricane P3215

Hit by a fighter over Portland, attempted to reach Warmwell airfield but crashed into a wood at Abbotsbury. A New Zealander, son of a doctor, he had learnt to fly while a student at Nelson College, becoming the youngest qualified pilot in Australasia. He came to England at his own expense in October 1930, and by 1932 was with 32 Squadron, later 30 Squadron in Iraq. With later periods at Calshot and then an instructor at Grantham, he was examining officer at Hendon in 1938. Took over 87 Squadron on 12 July 1940. Buried in Holy Trinity Churchyard, Warmwell. His parents were Dr John Lovell-Gregg MD & MrsDora L Lovell-Gregg of Picton, Marlborough, NZ.

18.05   P/O P W Comely RAF
              87 Sqn
              Hurricane P2872

Shot down into the sea by Me110 off Portland. He has no known grave. Joined the RAF in January 1939 and joined his first squadron, No.145, in October. In February 1940 he began ferrying Hurricanes to 87 Squadron in France, remaining with them in May. He was 19.

Victories:	20 May	Ju88	Destroyed
	20 May	Ju88	Destroyed
	7/8 Aug	He111	Destroyed
	11 Aug	Ju88	Destroyed
	15 Aug	Me110	Destroyed

18.15   P/O C H Hight RAF
              234 Sqn
              Hurricane R6988

Shot down by fighter near Bournemouth, Hight being killed as his parachute failed to deploy. Buried in Boscombe Cemetery. Being the only allied airman to die over Bournemouth in the war, a street was named Pilot Hight Road in North Bournemouth after the war. From Stratford, New Zealand, he had learnt to fly in 1937 and in 1938 had worked his passage to England to join the RAF. Once trained he was posted to 234 Squadron on 6 November 1939. Son of Herbert E & Mrs Emma Hight of Stratford, Taranaki, NZ.

18.50   P/O F W Cale RAF
              266 Sqn
              Spitfire N3168

Crashed in flames on the bank of the Medway River following combat action. Baled out into the river and died. From Western Australia he was accepted by a RAAF board for the RAF and sailed for England in early 1939. Joined 266 in early November 1939. Body recovered from the River at Teston and buried in the Westminster City Cemetery, Ealing. He was 25.

19.15   P/O J T Johnston RAF
            151 Sqn
            Hurricane P3941

Shot down over the Channel off Dymchurch by Me109. Picked up but died. A Canadian, he had joined the RAF in January 1939 and was posted to 151 on 13 July 1940. Aged 26 he was buried in Folkestone New Cemetery, Kent. Son of Peter & Mrs Alice Johnston of Brandon, Manitoba, Canada.

19.20   P/O M Rozwadowski
            151 Sqn
            Hurricane V7410

Missing after combat with Me109s over the Channel. Escaped from Poland after fighting with the PAF, and eventually reached England. Commissioned into the RAF in January 1940. Posted to 151 on 8 August. He was 25.

Victories   15 Aug   ½ Me109   Destroyed

Friday, 16 August

Another day of heavy air actions against RAF airfields and other targets. This day saw an action which brought Flight Lieutenant J B Nicholson of 249 Squadron the Victoria Cross, the only one awarded to an RAF fighter pilot during the war. His action has been well recorded, staying with his burning fighter while determined to attack the Me110 fighter that had attacked him before finally being forced to bale out. Some twenty-three RAF fighters were lost but several pilots survived bale outs. Another day of heavy losses for the Gemans, with well over forty aircraft lost.

12.35   S/L R L Wilkinson RAF
            266 Sqn
            Spitfire R6768

Collided with a Me109 of JG26 and crashed at Eastry Court, Deal. He had led his Squadron against a number of 109s of JG26, but they were in turn reinforced and 266 were decimated. Four Spitfires were shot down and another damaged. He came from Rotherfield, Sussex, entering the RAF College at Cranwell in early 1929. Becoming a pilot he was sent to No. 3 Squadron. In 1932 he was posted overseas, to Transjordan and Palestine, becoming PA to the AOC, Sir Wilfred Freeman, and in 1934 was made PA to AVM Cyril Newall (Chief of the Air Staff). Returning to the UK he became an instructor with the University Air Squadron at Cambridge then joined the staff at the CFS, Upavon, followed by a period at the Air Ministry. When war came he was posted to command 266 on 6 July 1940. Buried in Margate Cemetery, Kent. Son of Major Clement A Wilkinson (The King's Shropshire Light Infantry) & Mrs Ruth V E Wilkinson.

Victories:

12 Aug	Do17	Destroyed
15 Aug	Ju88	Destroyed
16 Aug	Me109	by collision

12.40   Sub-Lt H LaF Greenshields RNVR
266 Sqn
Spitfire N3240

Missing after combat with Me109s over the Channel, crashing in the suburbs of Calais, France. From Axminster, Devon, he was turned down by the RAF due to defective eyesight, but successfully became a pilot with the RNVR. Attached to the RAF and 266 on 1 July 1940. Claimed by JG26. Buried in the Calais Southern Cemetery, he was 22. Son of Major David J Greenshields, formaerly of the Royal Artillery, & Mrs Edmee Greenshields of Hawkchurch, Devon.

12.45   P/O N G Bowen RAF
266 Sqn
Spitfire N3095

Shot down by Me109 over Adisham, near Canterbury, Kent. He came from Wallington, Surrey, eldest son of the Rector of St Mary's Church there. Joined the RAF in February 1939 and posted to 266 in early 1940. He was aged 20 and buried in Wallingford Cemetery. His parents were the Revd. Herbert P & Mrs Stella M Bowen.

Victories:

2 Jun	Me109	Damaged
12 Aug	Ju88	Destroyed

12.45   F/L H M Ferriss RAF
111 Sqn
Hurricane R4193

Collided with a Do17 of 7./KG76 over Marden, Kent, crashing on Sheephurst Farm. From Lee, London he was with the University Air Squadron at London University, and later a medical student. Joined the RAF in July 1937, ending up with 111 on 7 May 1938, while the Squadron was testing the new Hurricane fighter. He was two weeks past his 21st birthday. His DFC was gazetted 21 June 1940. Son of Henry F & Mrs Violet E Ferriss of Petts Wood, Orpington, Kent.

HM Ferris is pictured on the left.

Victories:			
	8 Apr	½ He111	Probable
	10 Apr	sh/He111	Destroyed
	18 May	Me109	Destroyed
	18 May	Me109	Destroyed
	18 May	Me110	Damaged
	31 May	Me109	Destroyed
	6 Jun	Me109	Destroyed
	6 Jun	Me109	Destroyed
	10 Jul	sh/Do17	Destroyed
	10 Jul	Me109	Destroyed
	28 Jul	He59	Destroyed
	13 Aug	Do17	Destroyed
	13 Aug	Do17	Damaged
	15 Aug	Do17	Probable
	16 Aug	Do17	by collision

13.00   P/O J E P Laricheliere RAF
213 Sqn
Hurricane

Failed to return from combat off Portland. Canadian from Montreal, graduating from that city's University in 1933. Joined the RAF in August 1939 and ended up with 213 Squadron on 25 May after a brief spell with 504 Squadron. He was 27 and has no known grave.

Victories:

13 Aug	Ju88	Destroyed
13 Aug	Me110	Destroyed
13 Aug	Me109	Destroyed
15 Aug	Me109	Destroyed
15 Aug	Ju87	Destroyed
15 Aug	Me109	Destroyed

13.00   P/O W M L Fiske III RAFVR
601 Sqn
Hurricane P3358

Damaged by return fire from enemy aircraft, and force-landed in flames at Tangmere, badly burned. Died in hospital on the 17th. Born in Brooklyn, New York, the son of an international banker, he was educated at Cambridge University in the early 1930s and was a well known Olympic bob-sleigh competitor, winning two gold medals as well as being Captain of the US team. He also raced sport cars, winning the Cambridge to London race in his 8-litre Bentley. In 1938 he married the former Countess of Warwick, Rose Bassett. His parents were William & Mrs Beulah Fiske. Buried in St Mary and St Blaise Churchyard, Boxgrove, West Sussex. On 4 July 1941 the Secretary of State for Air, Sir Archibald Sinclair, unveiled a memorial plaque to Fiske in the crypt of St Paul's Cathedral in London.

Victories: 13 Aug   Ju88   Destroyed

13.55   P/O M A King RAF
249 Sqn
Hurricane P3616

Shot down by fighter over Southampton and baled out, but parachute collapsed during descent and King was killed. Joined the RAF in August 1939 and found himself in 249 Squadron on 9 June 1940. He is buried in All Saints Churchyard, Fawley, Hampshire. He was the 19-year-old son of George E King MB, B.Ch & Mrs Ivy E King of Mill Hill, Middlesex.

17.15   F/L W H C Warner AAF
610 Sqn
Spitfire R6802

Missing after combat with Me109s off Dungeness. Youngest son of Sir Lionel and Lady Warner, he being the GM of Mersey Docks and Harbour. Commissioned into 610 Squadron AAF in May 1937. He was 21 and has no known grave.

Victories: 15 Aug   Me109   Destroyed

17.30   P/O L L Pyman RAFVR
                 65 Sqn
                 Spitfire K9915

Missing from combat off Deal. Educated at Stowe and Jesus College Cambridge, where he was a member of the University Air Squadron, then joined the VR in January 1939. Posted to 65 on 20 July 1940. Body was washed up on French coast and buried in Calais Southern Cemetery, France. He was 23, son of Ronald L & Mrs Catherine F Pyman of Oxford.

Victories: 14 Aug   Me109   Destroyed

Saturday, 17 August

The past eight days had cost the RAF around 78 fighter pilots killed with nearly 30 more wounded. On this day the Air Staff sanctioned the transfer of twenty volunteer pilots from Fairey Battle units who were keen to help Fighter Command. Following a brief conversion course onto Spitfire or Hurricane, they began to be posted to various fighter squadrons during the second half of August.

No operational fatalities.

Sunday, 18 August

After a very quiet day on the 17th, the 18th saw mass attacks by the Luftwaffe. Again it was RAF airfields that took the brunt of these. Stuka dive-bombers were used but suffered heavy casualties, so heavy that they did not see further action until November. The airfields of Biggin Hill, Kenley and Croydon were hit, but so were several non-fighter airfields such as Gosport and Thorney Island. RAF Manston was strafed by a number of Me109s destroying two Spitfires and a Hurricane and wounding a number of RAF ground personnel, one fatally. In all over 40 RAF fighters were lost or destroyed, but once again it was the Germans who suffered most heavily, with 60 aircraft lost, 16 of which were Ju87s, and the same number of Me109s lost. Another dozen or so were Me110s.

13.05   P/O N D Solomon RAFVR
                 17 Sqn
                 Hurricane L1921

Missing after engagement with Me109s off Dover, falling into the sea. Body washed up on French coast and buried at Pihen-lès-Guînes. Joined the VR in the summer of 1938 and his first Squadron flew Blenheims (29) but later moved to single-seat fighters. Sent to 17 Squadron on 10 August 1940. Son of Archibald B & Mrs Ethel B Solomon of Birmingham.

13.18   F/L S D P Connors DFC RAF
              111 Sqn
              Hurricane R4187

Men of III Sqn. F/L Connors is pictured furthest on the right.

Hit by AA fire during attack on a Do17 that was bombing RAF Kenley, crashing at Wallington. He was 28 and is buried in North Berwick Cemetery. He had been born in Calcutta, India, but once in England he joined the AAF in March 1936. Posted to 111 Squadron in June 1938, which by May 1940 was operating patrols along the French coast. Appointed B Flight commander, his DFC was gazetted on 31 May. He was 28. Son of Pierce F J P & Mrs Muriel Connors, and husband of Mrs Majorie V Connors of North Berwick, Midlothian.

Victories:	18 May	Me109	Destroyed
	18 May	Ju88	Destroyed
	19 May	He111	Destroyed
	19 May	He111	Destroyed
	19 May	He111	Destroyed
	19 May	Ju88	Destroyed
	31 May	Me109	Probable
	2 Jun	He111	Probable
	7 Jun	Me109	Destroyed
	19 Jul	Me109	Destroyed
	25 Jul	Me109	Damaged
	31 Jul	sh/Ju88	Probable
	11 Aug	Me109	Destroyed
	15 Aug	Ju88	Damaged

15 Aug	Ju88	Destroyed
15 Aug	Me110	Destroyed
15 Aug	Me110	Damaged
16 Aug	Do17	Damaged
18 Aug	Do17	Destroyed

13.30   F/O F Gruszka
65 Sqn
Spitfire R6713

Crashed at Westbere, near Canterbury during patrol. Buried in Northwood Cemetery, Middlesex. He was aged 30 and had been in the Polish Air Force before the war, and before escaping to England.

13.30   Sgt P K Walley AAF
615 Sqn
Hurricane P2768

Shot up in combat by Me109 of JG3. Died attempting to crashland on Morden Park golf course, rather than baling out over a populated area. From Barnes he was an apprentice tool maker, joining the AAF as an aircraft hand and air gunner with 615 Squadron in March 1938. Selected for pilot training as the war began. Once trained he returned to 615 on 6 August. He was 20 and was buried in St Luke's Churchyard, Whyteleaf, Surrey.

Victories: 16 Aug   sh/Me109   Probable

13.35   P/O J W Bland RAF
501 Sqn
Hurricane P3208

Shot down by Oblt. G Schöphel of JG26, crashing at Calcott Hill, Surrey. Buried in Gravesend Cemetery, Kent. Joined AAF before the war, commissioned in June 1939. He then joined 601 Squadron but moved to 501 on 12 July 1940. He was 30 years old. Son of Thomas H Bland BA & Mrs Margaret A Bland of St Matthew's Vicarage, Cotham Park, Bristol.

Victories: 11 Jul   sh/Do17   Destroyed
29 Jul   Ju87   Destroyed

14.15   Sgt L N Guy RAFVR
             601 Sqn
             Hurricane R4191

Shot down by JG27 over Sussex Coast, he has no known grave. Joined the VR in August 1939 and was with 601 by early July 1940. He has no known grave and was the 25-year-old son of Leonard & Mrs Ethel Guy of Weston-super-Mare, Somerset. Having used all his ammunition shooting down a Ju87 on 16 August he said the second Stuka had gone into the sea trying to avoid his dummy attacks.

Victories:	11 Jul	Ju87	Probable
	11 Jul	Ju87	Damaged
	11 Aug	He111	Probable
	11 Aug	He111	Probable
	11 Aug	He111	Damaged
	13 Aug	Me110	Destroyed
	13 Aug	½ Me110	Destroyed
	13 Aug	Me110	Damaged
	15 Aug	½ Ju88	Destroyed
	16 Aug	Ju87	Destroyed
	16 Aug	Ju87	Destroyed

14.50   Sgt R P Hawkings RAFVR
             601 Sqn
             Hurricane L1990

Shot down by Uffz. Born of JG27, falling near Pagham. Buried in St Peter's Churchyard, Filton. Son of Redvers A & Mrs Emily A Hawkings of Filton, Bristol. Had joined the VR in the summer of 1939 and completed his training when war came. Posted to 601 in June 1940.

Victories:	7 Jul	sh/Do17	Destroyed
	11 Jul	He111	Probable
	11 Aug	Me110	Destroyed
	13 Aug	Ju88	Destroyed
	13 Aug	Ju88	Probable

17.30   P/O J B Ramsay RAF
             151 Sqn
             Hurricane R4181

Failed to return from combat over Chelmsford, crashing at Burnham-on-Crouch. Buried in Brookwood Military Cemetery, the son of C Allan & Mrs Esme S Ramsay of Lilliput, Dorsetshire. Born in India he joined the RAF in July

1938. In May 1939 he went to No. 24 (Communication) Squadron at Hendon and saw service in France in 1940. Converting to fighters he was posted to 151 on 29 July. Originally he was recorded as missing and his name is on the Runnymede Memorial but after the war an Essex crash site was excavated which found his remains still in the cockpit. These were buried in Brookwood Military Cemetery in 1983.

17.46   F/L G E B Stoney RAF (pictured fourth from left)
              501 Sqn
              Hurricane P2549

Shot down by Me109 over the Thames Estuary, falling near Chilham. Buried in St Helen's Churchyard, Sefton. Joined the RAF in August 1929 and by 1930 was an instructor with 504 Squadron. He then went to No. 4 (Army Co-Operation) Squadron in 1932 before going on to the Reserve. Recalled when the war started he went to 501 Squadron on 28 July 1940 as a flight commander. His parents were E Bowes & Mrs K M Stoney; husband to Aileen B Stoney of West Derby, Liverpool. He was 29 years old. Probably shot down by Hptm. J Foesoe of JG51.

Victories:	29 Jul	Ju87	Destroyed
	12 Aug	Me110	Damaged
	15 Aug	2/Ju87s	Destroyed
	15 Aug	2/Ju87s	Damaged

17.50   F/O R H A Lee DSO DFC RAF
85 Sqn
Hurricane P2923

Last seen in pursuit of enemy aircraft thirty miles off the east coast. He has no known grave. Born in London, he was 23 and after his studies at Charterhouse School, went to the RAF College, Cranwell in 1935-37. Joined 85 Squadron in June 1938, going to France with it when war began. Awarded the DFC, gazetted 8 March 1940, followed by the DSO, gazetted 31 May 1940.

Victories:	21 Nov '39	He111	Destroyed
	10 May	Hs126	Destroyed
	10 May	sh/Ju86	Destroyed
	10 May	Ju88	Damaged
	11 May	EA	Destroyed
	11 May	EA	Destroyed

(but believed to have destroyed nine enemy aircraft)

Monday, 19 August

This day saw the commencement of the Luftwaffe's plans to attack British aircraft factories. According to their intelligence reports Fighter Command should have been down to its reserves of aircraft, and by destroying factories, reinforcements would be delayed or even stopped.

11.30   Sgt J H Round RAFVR
Sgt W H Want RAFVR
Sgt M P Digby-Worsley RAF
248 Sqn
Blenheim L9457

Failed to return from reconnaissance sortie to Norwegian coast. Round came from Netherton Dudley, Worcs, was 27, son of John H & Mrs Beatrice E Round, of Netherton. Digby-Worsley came from Hornsey, Middlesex, aged 18, adopted son of Inez G Digby-Worsley. Want was 28.

17.20   P/O J A P Studd RAF
66 Sqn
Spitfire N3182

Crashed off Orfordness during engagement with He111. Baled out and rescued by the Aldeburgh lifeboat but did not regain consciousness. From Paignton, Devon, at one time he was PA to AVM T Leigh Mallory. Aged 22, he is buried in Holy Trinity

Churchyard, Touchen End, Berkshire. Son of Vivian M & Mrs Olivette Studd of Paignton, Devon.

Victories: 29 Jul   sh/He111   Destroyed

Tuesday, 20 August

Today saw the famous speech to Parliament by the British Prime Minister, Winston Churchill. His 'Never in the field of human conflict has so much been owed, by so many, to so few' would go down in history, and the pilots of Fighter Command during this summer, became forever, The Few.

13.45   Mid. P J Patterson FAA
               242 Sqn
               Hurricane P2967

Dived into the sea and exploded five miles north-east of Winterton, Humberside, during a patrol, cause unknown. No known grave, aged 29. Loaned to the RAF on 15 June 1940, and posted to 242 Squadron on 1 July. Son of Horace J & Mrs Nellie T Patterson of Southbourne, Hampshire.

Wednesday, 21 August

No operational fatalities

Thursday, 22 August

13.15   Sgt G R Collett RAFVR
               54 Sqn
               Spitfire R6708

Shot down by fighters off Deal. Body recovered and buried in Bergen-op-Zoom War Cemetery, Netherlands. He was 24. His parents were George C & Mrs Elizabeth M Collett of Luton, Bedfordshire. Joined the VR in March 1939, going to 54 Squadron on 15 July.

Victories: 24 Jul   Me109   Destroyed

19.35   Sgt M Keymer RAFVR
              65 Sqn
              Spitfire K9909

Shot down by Ltn H Krug of 4/JG26 or Oblt. G Schöpfel of 9/JG26 off Dover. Born Eastleigh, Hants, he was 24. His body was recovered and buried in Bazinghen Churchyard, France. His parents were Bernard Wm & Mrs Ellen C Keymer of Farnham, Surrey. They also lost another son John G Keymer on 10 May 1941, a Wellington pilot with 149 Squadron, during a raid on Hamburg. Joined 65 on 7 August. Pre-war he had been a member of the Civil Air Guard, joining the RAFVR in June 1939.

Victories: 14 Aug   sh/Me109   Destroyed

Friday, 23 August

No operational fatalities

On the 23rd the German High Command ordered the start of attacks on British airfields. The obvious ones would be those of Fighter Command in the south of England, but it became clear that they did not know exactly which airfields were fighter bases, and a number of other types of aerodromes were also to be targets.

On this night of 23/24 August, German bombs fell on London, said to have been by mistake. However, this proved to be the start of Britain's campaign against German towns and cities, including its capital, Berlin. Therefore, Phase Three of the Battle began at this time.

Saturday, 24 August

After bad weather in the morning, attacks that then developed concentrated on airfields in the south-east of England, in order to finally knock out Fighter Command.

10.15   P/O P Zenker
              501 Sqn
              Hurricane P3141

Missing in action north-west of Dover. No known grave. Aged 25, he flew in Poland with 142 Squadron. Joined 501 on 7 August. His name is on the Polish Air Force Memorial at Northolt.

Victories: 3 Sep '39   Hs126   Destroyed
                  12 Aug   Ju87   Destroyed
                  18 Aug   Me109   Destroyed

12.40   S/L P A Hunter DSO RAF (pictured top)
P/O F H King DFM RAF (pictured bottom)
264 Sqn
Defiant N1535

Shot down during attack on formation of Ju88s. No known graves. Hunter came from Cheshum, Bucks, leaving a wife Eleanor M Hunter. His parents were Albert and Clare Hunter. He was aged 27. Joined the RAF in 1931, seeing service in the Middle East before going to Cranwell and then being on the staff at the Central Flying School. DSO 14 June 1940. King, from Leicester, was 24, and had joined the RAF in 1935. Their successes were mostly over the Dunkirk evacuation. King was awarded the DFM on 14 June 1940.

Victories:	12 May	Ju88	Destroyed
	27 May	Me109	Destroyed
	27 May	½ He111	Destroyed
	28 May	Me109	Destroyed
	28 May	Me109	Destroyed
	29 May	Me109	Destroyed
	29 May	EA	Destroyed
	29 May	Ju87	Destroyed
	31 May	Me109	Destroyed
	31 May	He111	Destroyed
	31 May	He111	Destroyed

12.40   P/O J T Jones RAFVR
P/O W A Ponting RAF (pictured)
264 Sqn
Defiant L6966

Shot down by Maj. G Lützow Kdr. of JG3 over the Channel. No known graves. Jones was the son of Francis L & Mrs Florence M Jones, and was 21. Ponting came from Whetstone, Middlesex, aged 30, son of Robert & Mrs Ada Ponting.

12.45   F/O I G Shaw RAF
Sgt A Berry RAF (pictured)
264 Sqn
Defiant L7027

Shot down by Mj. G Lützow, Kdr. JG3 over the Channel. No known graves. Shaw came from Norwood, Surrey, son of Angus B & Mrs Minnie Shaw. 23-year-old Berry was from Longsight, Manchester, son of Walter & Mrs Jane Berry, and husband to May.

16.00   P/O R S Gaskell (Safe)
Sgt W H Machin RAF (pictured)
264 Sqn
Defiant L6965

Shot down by Me109 of JG51. Gaskell slightly wounded while Machin, aged 20, and from Handsworth, Birmingham, died of wounds. He is buried in his home town. Parents were Edmund W & Mrs Ivy M Machin.

16.45   P/O D N Woodger RAF (pictured left)
Sgt D L Wright (pictured right)
235 Sqn
Blenheim T1804

Shot down by Hurricane of No.1 RCAF Squadron and crashed into Bracklesham Bay, West Sussex. Woodger came from Coulsdon, Surrey, was 20, and has no known grave. Son of Reginald W & Mrs Edith M Woodger. Wright, from Lichfield, Staffs, was 18, son of William & Mrs Mary A Wright, living in Chasetown, Staffs, and is buried in St Ann's Churchyard, Chasetown, Burtonwood, Staffordshire.

Sunday, 25 August

17.30   P/O R M Hogg RAF
152 Sqn
Spitfire R6810

Shot down by German fighters over the Channel. From Gorey, Jersey, C.I. He has no known grave. 21-year-old son of Cmdr. Philip J Hogg DSC RNR & Mrs Kathleen Hogg. Flight Cadet at Cranwell in April 1938 he had gone to 145 Squadron in October 1939. Early in July 1940 he moved to 152 Squadron.

Victories:	18 Jul	Do17	Damaged
	25 Jul	sh/Do17	Destroyed
	25 Jul	sh/Ju87	Destroyed
	8 Aug	Me109	Destroyed
	8 Aug	Me109	Probable
	12 Aug	sh/2/Ju88s	Probables
	12 Aug	sh/Ju88	Destroyed
	21 Aug	sh/Ju88	Destroyed
	23 Aug	sh/Ju88	Destroyed

August 1940

17.30   P/O T S Wildblood RAF
152 Sqn
Spitfire R6994

Failed to return after fight with fighters over the Channel. Born in Egypt, the son of Brig. F H Wildblood DSO, and won a King's cadetship to RAF Cranwell in 1938. Joined 152 in October 1939. He was 20 years old and has no known grave. Was mentioned in despatches, 17 March 1941.

Victories	27 Feb	½ He111	Destroyed
	11 Aug	Me109	Destroyed
	12 Aug	Me110	Destroyed
	12 Aug	Ju87	Destroyed
	18 Aug	sh/Ju87	Destroyed

17.30   P/O J A L Philippart RAFVR
213 Sqn
Hurricane V7226

Shot down by Maj. H Meyer, Gr.Kdr. I/JG53. Baled out but died. Body washed ashore on the 28th, and buried Exeter Higher Cemetery. Exhumed and repatriated to the Pelouse d'Honneur Cemetery, Brussels, Belgium in 1949. He was 31 and from Mont-St-Guibert, Belgium. He joined 213 on 23 July having escaped from his native country in June.

Victories:	11 Aug	Ju88	Destroyed
	15 Aug	Me109	Destroyed
	15 Aug	Me109	Destroyed
	15 Aug	Me109	Destroyed
	15 Aug	Me110	Probable
	22 Aug	Ju88	Destroyed
	25 Aug	Ju88	Destroyed

18.00   P/O H D Atkinson DFC RAF
213 Sqn
Hurricane P3200

Missing after combat over Warmwell. From Wintringham, Yorkshire, he was 22 and a graduate of RAF College Cranwell, where he also excelled at cricket. Body recovered from the sea and buried in Market Weighton Cemetery, Yorkshire. Parents were Fred & Mrs Adelaide Jane Atkinson of Scarborough. DFC 25 June 1940.

Victories:	19 May	He111	Destroyed
	19 May	Do17	Damaged
	19 May	sh/Hs126	Destroyed

20 May	sh/Do17	Destroyed
20 May	sh/Hs126	Destroyed
20 May	Me110	Probable
27 May	Me109	Destroyed
28 May	Me109	Destroyed
29 May	He111	Probable
29 May	½ Ju88	Damaged
12 Aug	Me110	Destroyed
12 Aug	Me110	Destroyed
13 Aug	Me110	Destroyed
14 Aug	He111	Destroyed
16 Aug	Me109	Destroyed
18 Aug	Me109	Destroyed

17.45 S/L C W Williams RAF (pictured second from right)
17 Sqd
Hurricane R4199

Shot down in head-on attack with Me110, and crashed into the sea off Portland. From South Wales, he was aged 30. No known grave. He had joined the RAF in 1926 as an apprentice/fitter. Won a Cranwell cadetship and served with 32 and 84 Squadrons pre-war. Staff College 1936 and Air Ministry 1938. Took command of 17 Squadron on 18 July 1940. Son of Mrs Ada Williams, husband of Nell Williams. They had one son.

Victories:	18 Aug	Do17	Destroyed
	21 Aug	sh/Ju88	Destroyed
	21 Aug	sh/Ju88	Destroyed
	24 Aug	He111	Destroyed
	25 Aug	Me110	Destroyed

18.05   Sgt S R E Wakeling RAFVR
              87 Sqn
              Hurricane V7250

Shot down over Portland, crashing at New Barn, outside Dorchester. Buried in Holy Trinity Churchyard, Warmwell. Aged 21 and son of James and Jessie Wakeling. He had joined the VR in the spring of 1939, joining 87 in early July 1940.

19.00   P/O K R Gillman RAF (pictured in the middle)
              32 Sqn
              Hurricane N2433

Missing after combat off Dover. From Dover, this 19-year-old has no known grave. Son to Richard G & Mrs Gladys A Gillman of River, Kent. Joined the RAF in March 1939 and after training went to 32 Squadron on 10 May 1940.

Victories: 19 Jul   Me109   Destroyed

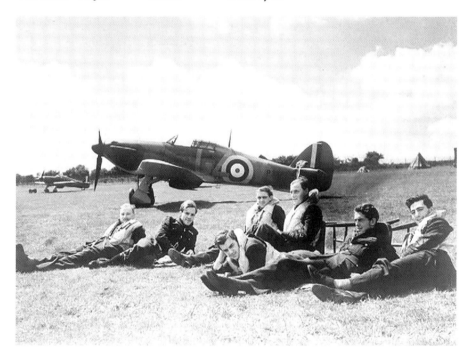

19.00   Sgt T E Westmoreland RAFVR (pictured bottom left)
616 Sqn
Spitfire R6966

Last seen during combat over Canterbury. From Hudderfield, Yorkshire, he was 27, has no known grave. Son of Thomas G & Mrs Annie Westmoreland. Joined the VR in May 1938 and went to 616 Squadon in July 1940.

Victories: 15 Aug   Ju88   Destroyed

22.00   P/O R A Rhodes RAF
Sgt R J Gouldstone AAF (pictured)
AC2 N Jacobson RAFVR
29 Sqn
Blenheim L1330

Shot down in combat with a He111 over Wainfleet, near Spurn Head. Rhodes was 19. Gladstone, from Ryarsh, Kent, was also 19, and Jacobson, 18, was from Grimsby. All were killed. Rhodes has no known grave but Gladstone is buried in St Martin's Churchyard, Ryarsh, where his parents, Frederick J & Mrs Lillian Gouldstone lived. Jacobson's body was picked up by a trawler and buried at sea. He was the son of Alfred E & Mrs Olive Jacobson.

Victories: 18 Aug   He111   Destroyed (Rhodes)

?	Sgt C Haigh RAF
	Sgt J G B Fletcher AAF
	LAC A L Austin RAFVR
	604 Sqn
	Blenheim L6782

Crashed near Witheridge, Exeter during night patrol. Haigh, 23, was buried in St Margaret's Churchyard, Swinton, Yorkshire. Fletcher, from Wadhurst, Sussex, aged 20, was buried in Forest Row Cemetery, Sussex. Son of John G & Mrs Elsie E Fletcher and husband of Mrs Joyce Fletcher. Austin, 25, was buried in Northwood Cemetery, Middlesex.

Monday, 26 August

12.15	Sgt M Ridley RAF
	616 Sqn
	Spitfire R6633

Shot down by Hptm. J Foezoe of 4/JG51 over Dover. From Benwell, Newcastle-upon-Tyne, he was 24 years old. Buried in Folkestone New Cemetery, Kent. Parents were Mr M and Mrs Isabel Ridley. Joined the RAF in January 1931 as an apprentice, graduating as a fitter/airframes in 1933. Selected for pilot training he went to 616 in early 1940. Over Dunkirk on 28 May he was slightly wounded but got home.

12.15	F/O G E Moberly AAF
	616 Sqn
	Spitfire N3275

Shot down by Hptm. J Foezoe of 4/JG51 off Dover. Born in Bombay, India he was 25. His body was recovered and buried in St Mary's Churchyard, Caterham-on-the-Hill, Surrey. Son to Charles N & Mrs Kate C Moberly of Folkestone, Kent. Learnt to fly in 1937 and joined 609 AAF Squadron in 1938. He had been among the first to go to 616 Squadron when it was formed that November. Saw action over Dunkirk.

Victories:	28 May	Me109	Destroyed
	28 May	Me109	Probable
	1 Jun	Ju88	Destroyed
	3 Jul	sh/Do17	Destroyed
	15 Aug	Ju88	Destroyed
	25 Aug	Me109	Destroyed

12.26   F/L A J Banham (Safe)
             Sgt B Baker RAFVR (pictured)
             264 Sqn
             Defiant L6985

Shot down by Me109 over Thanet after action against Do17s. Banham baled out and was rescued from the sea but Baker was lost. From Kings Norton, Birmingham, he was 27 and has no known grave. Son of Walter H V & Mrs Gertrude Baker, husband of Ethel Baker of King's Norton, Birmingham.

Victories: 26 Aug   Do17   Destroyed

Banham is pictured here on the bottom row, fourth from the left.

12.26   F/O I R Stephenson (Safe)
             Sgt W Maxwell RAFVR (pictured)
             264 Sqn
             Defiant L7025

Shot down by Me109 two miles off Herne Bay. Stephenson baled out and was rescued from the sea but Maxwell was lost. He came from Meols, Cheshire, aged 23 but has no known grave. Son of William and Mrs Maud Maxwell.

12.40   P/O F K Webster RAFVR
             610 Sqn
             Spitfire R6595

Damaged in combat, crashed attempting to land at RAF Hawkinge. He was 26 and is buried in Sandown Cemetery, Isle of Wight. Family from Lake, IoW. Joined the VR in April 1939, and posted to 610 Squadron on 28 July.

15.30   F/O R L Edwards RCAF
1 (RCAF) Sqn
Hurricane P3874

Shot down by Do17z of 7/KG2 following attack upon RAF Debden, and crashed at The Hydes, Little Bradfield. Buried in Brookwood Military Cemetery; aged 28.

Tuesday, 27 August

12.00   P/O C J Arthur RAF (pictured left)
Sgt E A Ringwood RAF
Sgt R C R Cox RAFVR (pictured right)
248 Sqn
Blenheim L9449

Failed to return from reconnaissance mission to Norwegian coast. Arthur came from Radyr, Glamorgan, aged 22, son of James F & Mrs Margaret E Arthur. Ringwood was 20. They have no known graves. Cox's body was washed ashore in Sweden and is buried in Kriberg

Cemetery, Gothenberg. Aged 30, he was the son of Harry & Mrs Eva Cox of Luton, Bedfordshire, and husband of Mrs Violet M Cox, also of Luton.

12.58   Sub-Lt W J M Moss RN
213 Sqn
Hurricane N2336

Lost control and hit the sea during routine patrol. He was 22 and has no known grave. Son of William E & Mrs Mary S Cox of Newton Abbot, Devon. Joined 213 on 1 July.

Wednesday, 28 August

08.55   P/O D Whitley RAF
Sgt R C Turner RAFVR
264 Sqn
Defiant N5174

Shot down by JG26 over Thanet, crashing in Kingswood Challock Forest. Whitley was 21 and is buried in Bedford Cemetery. Son of David E & Mrs Olivia Whitley of Kilburn, Middlesex. Turner, from Reading, was the son of George H & Mrs Ethel K Turner of Reading, Berkshire. He was 25 and is buried in Henley Road Cemetery, Berkshire.

Turner is pictured top row, second from left.

Victories (Whitley):	24 May	½ Me110	Destroyed
	27 May	sh/He111	Destroyed
	29 May	Ju87	Destroyed
	29 May	Ju87	Destroyed
	29 May	Ju87	Destroyed
	15 Aug	He111	Probable
	24 Aug	Ju88	Destroyed

Whitley is pictured on the far right.

08.55   P/O P L Kenner RAFVR (pictured left)
           P/O C E Johnson RAFVR (pictured right)
           264 Sqn
           Defiant L7026

Shot down by JG26 over Thanet, crashing on Sillibourne Farm, Hinxshill. Kenner was 21 and is buried in London Road, Brentwood, Essex. Son of Thomas W & Mrs Gladys Kenner of Brentwood, Essex. His brother, Sgt J W Kenner, was killed with 37 Squadron on 29 May 1941.

Johnson was 31 and is buried in Folkestone New Cemetery, Kent. It was his first operational sortie. His brother Louis survived three bomber tours, receiving the DFC & Bar. His parents were Charles H & Mrs Helen Johnson and he was husband to Mrs Doris E Johnson, of Bridgford, Nottingham.

09.20   S/L G D Garvin (safe)
           F/L R C V Ash RAF
           264 Sqn
           Defiant L7021

Shot down by Me109, falling on Luddenham Marsh, Faversham, Kent. Both men baled out but Ash had been mortally wounded in the air and did not survive. He was 31 and is buried in Western Cemetery, St Andrews, Fife, Scotland. Son of Robert C Ash MC MD & Mrs Mennie Ash of St Andrews.

Victories:	24 Aug	Ju88	Destroyed (Garvin)
	24 Aug	Ju88	Destroyed

16.45   F/L J L G Cunningham AAF
           603 Sqn
           Spitfire R6751

Lost in combat with Me109s over Dover. From Burntisland, Fife, he was 23 years old and has no known grave. Son of Thomas & Mrs Jessie Cunningham.

Victories:	7 Dec '39	He111	Damaged
	20 Jul	sh/Do17	Destroyed

16.45   P/O D K MacDonald RAFVR
603 Sqn
Spitfire L1046

Missing after combat with Me109s over Dover. Aged 22, from Murrayfield, Edinburgh, he has no known grave. Son of James H & Mrs Isa M MacDonald.

17.00   P/O K H Cox RAFVR
610 Sqn
Spitfire P9511

Shot down by Me109 during combat over Dover, crashing inland at Stelling Minnis, Kent. He was 24 and was cremated at Birmingham Municipal Crematorium, his ashes being scattered on Old Castle Bromwich aerodrome. Son of Henry & Mrs Beatrice Cox of King's Heath, Birmingham.

Victories:	12 Aug	Me109	Destroyed
	15 Aug	Me109	Probable
	18 Aug	Me109	Destroyed
	18 Aug	Do17	Probable

20.30   P/O N J V Benson RAF
603 Sqn
Spitfire N3105

Shot down by Me109 on Great Hay Farm, Leigh Green, Tenterden, Kent. He was 21 and is buried in St Mary's Churchyard, Great Ouseburn, Yorkshire. Son of Joseph M & Mrs Olive M Benson of Great Ouseburn.

Thursday, 29 August

16.00   Sgt E Manton AAF
610 Sqn
Spitfire R6629

Shot down in combat over Mayfield, Surrey, crashing near Gatwick. He came from Bebington, Cheshire, aged 25 and is buried in Hawkhurst Cemetery, Kent. Son of Edward F & Mrs Sarah Manton. AAF since 1935 as air gunner on Hawker biplanes, while also working as a postman.

18.15   F/L H R Hamilton RAF
          85 Sqn
          Hurricane V6623

Shot down by Me109 near Winchelsea, crashing near the ruins of Camber Castle, Sussex. A Canadian from Oak Point, King's Country, New Brunswick, he was 23, son of Wesley W & Mrs Nina P Hamilton. Buried in Folkestone New Cemetery, Kent. Earlier with 611 Squadron until 25 May 1940.

Victories:	30 Jul	sh/Me110	Destroyed
	18 Aug	Me110	Destroyed
	18 Aug	sh/He111	Destroyed
	29 Aug	Me109	Destroyed

Friday, 30 August

11.15   P/O C D Francis RAF
          253 Sqn
          Hurricane L1965

Shot down by Me109 near Percival Farm, Wrotham, Kent. From Stoke D'Abernon, Surrey, he was 19 and buried in Brookwood Military Cemetery in 1981, his body having lain undiscovered until then. Son of Frank Warner & Mrs Emmie Francis. Squadron moved down from Scotland on the 29th and this had been his first operational sortie.

11.20   P/O D N O Jenkins RAF
          253 Sqn
          Hurricane P3921

Shot down by Me109, crashed at Woldingham, Surrey. Baled out but killed by fighter on the way down. Aged 21 he is buried in St Margaret's Churchyard, Bagendon, Gloucestershire. Son of Revd. William O Jankins DD & Mrs Horatia M Jenkins of St Andrews, Fife, Scotland.

11.50   Sgt D Noble RAFVR
          43 Sqn
          Hurricane P3179

Shot down by Me109 over the Sussex coast, and crashed at Hove. Noble was 20 and came from East Retford, Nottinghamshire. What purported to be his remains were buried in East Retford Cemetery but excavating his fighter in 1996, his body was discovered and subsequently interred in the original grave. Son of Harry & Mrs Annie Noble of Retford.

Victories: 16 Aug   Ju87   Destroyed

11.51   S/L E B King RAF
              151 Sqn
              Hurricane V7369

Crashed during patrol near Strood, Kent, possibly due to enemy action. From Dublin, King was 29 and was buried in Highgate Cemetery, London. His parents were Sydney R & Mrs Kate E King of Bournemouth, Hampshire.

12.02   F/O J S Bell AAF
              616 Sqn
              Spitfire X4248

Shot down by Me109 over West Malling. Aged 23 he was buried in St Peter's Cemetery, Eastgate, Lincoln. Son of Major Herbert A Bell & Mrs Ethel M Bell of Lincoln. Bell was a BA (Cantab) from Charterhouse School.

Victories: 1 Jun   Me109   Destroyed
              ? Jun   He59   Damaged
              1 Jul   sh/He111   Damaged

16.00   Sgt F Gmur
              151 Sqn
              Hurricane R4213

Shot down over the Thames Estuary, crashing near Epping Green. He was Polish, aged 25, and is buried in Epping Cemetery, Essex. Had seen action over Poland with the 161st Squadron. Joined 151 RAF on 21 August 1940.

Victories: ? Sep   He111   Damaged

16.02   Sgt J I Johnson RAF
              222 Sqn
              Spitfire R6628

Shot down by Me109, crashing at Longhampark Lodge, Bishopsbourne, Kent. He was 26 and is buried in Towcaster Cemetery, Northamptonshire. Son of John I & Mrs Ellen A Johnson of Leicester.

17.15   Sgt J H Dickinson RAFVR
             253 Sqn
             Hurricane P3213

Shot down by Fw. D Koch of 5/JG26 over Dungeness, crashing near Woodchurch. Baled out but thought to have been killed in his parachute. He was 21 and buried in St Mary's Churchyard, Egton-with-Newland, Lancashire. Son of Norman & Mrs Mary Dickinson of Southport.

17.35   S/L J V C Badger DFC RAF
             43 Sqn
             Hurricane V6548

Crashed south of Woodchurch, Kent, after combat with Me109s. Badger suffered serious wounds and finally succumbed to them on 30 June 1941. He came from Lambeth, South London and was 29 when he died. He is buried in St Michael and All Angels Churchyard, Halton, Buckinghamshire. Awarded the Sword of Honour RAF College, Cranwell, 14 July 1933. His parents were John & Mrs Violet Badger, of Belfast, Northern Ireland.

Victories:	12 Jul	sh/He111	Destroyed
	21 Jul	Do17	Destroyed
	21 Jul	Do17	Destroyed
	8 Aug	Me109	Probable
	13 Aug	Ju88	Damaged
	13 Aug	Ju88	Damaged
	14 Aug	Ju88	Destroyed
	14 Aug	Ju88	Destroyed
	16 Aug	Ju87	Destroyed
	16 Aug	Ju87	Destroyed
	16 Aug	Ju87	Destroyed
	26 Aug	He111	Destroyed
	26 Aug	½ He111	Destroyed

Saturday, 31 August

Today Fighter Command had its heaviest losses to date. RAF Debden was hit by 100 bombs. In the meantime, six of the seven main RAF 11 Group bases were also hit badly.

08.25   S/L H M Starr RAF
253 Sqn
Hurricane P3115

Shot down by fighters, falling dead at Hamill Brickworks, near Eastry, having been shot in his parachute. He came from Swindon, Wiltshire, aged 25, and is buried in Radnor Street Cemetery, Swindon. Joined the RAF in 1934.

08.45   P/O R A C Aeberhardt RAF
19 Sqn
Spitfire R6895

Hydraulics damaged in combat which caused the Spitfire to overturn upon landing. Pilot killed. He was from Walton on Thames, aged 19 and is buried in Whittlesford (St Mary & St Andrew) Churchyard, Cambridgeshire.

08.45   F/L P S Weaver DFC RAF
56 Sqn
Hurricane V7378

Shot down by fighters over Colchester, crashing into the River Blackwater at West Point, Osea Island. Came from Chippenham, Wiltshire and was 22. He has no known grave. Son of Ernest N & Mrs Katharine H Weaver of Chippenham, Wiltshire. DFC gazetted on 1 October.

Victories:	20 Jul	sh/Ju88	Destroyed
	29 Jul	Me109	Destroyed
	12 Aug	Do17	Destroyed
	13 Aug	Me110	Destroyed
	13 Aug	Me110	Damaged
	16 Aug	½ Do17	Destroyed
	18 Aug	Me110	Destroyed
	18 Aug	He111	Destroyed
	24 Aug	He111	Destroyed
	28 Aug	Me109	Destroyed

13.30   P/O J Štěrbáček
310 Sqn
Hurricane P3159

Shot down by Me109 over Thames Estuary, crashing near Romford. From Blansko (born in Dolni Lhota), Czechoslovakia, aged 27, he was originally posted as missing. Now known to have crashed near Romford, his remains were buried in Brookwood Military Cemetery.

13.35   F/O M D Doulton AAF
601 Sqn
Hurricane R4215

Shot down by Me109 over the Thames Estuary. Originally thought to have crashed into the sea, his remains were located in 1984, having crashed near Wennington Church, near Romford. He was cremated in Hastings, Sussex and the ashes were interred in Salehurst Church, East Sussex. He was 31. Son of Orrok M & Mrs Catherine M Doulton, and husband of Mrs Carol Doulton of Vinehall, Sussex, who was a WRAF Mechanic.

Victories:	11 Jul	sh/Do17	Destroyed
	20 Jul	He59	Destroyed
	13 Aug	Ju88	Probable
	13 Aug	Me110	Damaged
	15 Aug	sh/Ju88	Destroyed
	16 Aug	Ju87	Destroyed
	16 Aug	2/Ju87s	Damaged

16.00   Sgt H A Bolton RAFVR
79 Sqn
Hurricane V7200

Damaged in combat near Kenley aerodrome, crashed attempting a crash landing at Haliloo Farm, Warlingham. He came from West Hartlepool, was aged 21, and is buried in Stranton Cemetery, Hartepool. Son of Herbert S & Mrs Margaret Bolton of West Hartlepool.

18.30   F/O R McG Waterston AAF
603 Sqn
Spitfire X4273

Aircraft spun down after combat with Me109s over Woolwich, falling near Repository Road. Possibly shot down by I/JG3. He was 23 and was cremated at Warriston Crematorium, Edinburgh. Son of James S & Mrs Mabel Waterston of Edinburgh.

Victories:	30 Aug	Me109	Destroyed

19.10   F/O E J Wilcox RAF
72 Sqn
Spitfire P9457

Shot down over Dungeness and crashed at Hungerford Field, Chickenden Farm, Staplehurst, Kent. From Mitcham, Surrey, aged 23, he is buried in All Saint's Churchyard, Staplehurst. Son of Ernest J & Mrs Grace A Wilcox.

Victories: 1 Jun   Ju87   Destroyed
                    1 Jul   sh/He59   Destroyed

September 1940

Sunday, 1 September

11.15   F/O O StJ Pigg RAF
              72 Sqn
              Spitfire P9458

Shot down by Me109 at Elvey Farm, Pluckley, west of Ashford. He was 22 years of age, he is buried in St Peter's Burial Ground, Durham. Son of the Revd. John J Pigg and Mrs Mabel T Pigg of Chatton Vicarage, Northumberland. Had joined the RAF in March 1937 and posted to 72 Squadron from November 1937.

Victories: 2 Jun   Ju87   Destroyed
                 15 Aug   Me109   Destroyed

11.30   F/Sgt F G Berry DFM RAF
              1 Sqn
              Hurricane P3276

Shot down at Brisley Farm, Ruckinge, south of Ashford, by Me109. Born Calcutta, India, the son of a soldier. He was 26 and is buried in Pinner New Cemetery, Harrow, Middlesex. DFM 20 August 1940. Had been a Halton Apprentice in 1935 and later applied for pilot training. Believed to have claimed six enemy aircraft destroyed, two probably destroyed and three damaged.

Known victories: 20 Apr   Me109   Probable
                       17 Jun   He111   Destroyed
                       16 Aug   He111   Destroyed

14.00   P/O J K G Clifton RAF
              253 Sqn
              Hurricane P5185

Shot down in combat over Dungeness and crashed at Grave Lane, Staplehurst, Kent. Born in Plymouth, he was 21 and is buried in St John's Churchyard, Staplegrove, Somerset. Son of John H & Mrs Susie D A Clifton of Taunton, having moved there in 1928. He had joined the RAF in February 1939, posted to 253 in November.

Victories: 18 May   Do17   Destroyed
                 19 May   Me109   Probable
                 31 Aug   He111   Destroyed

14.15   Sgt G B Booth RAFVR
         85 Sqn
         Hurricane L2071

Shot down in combat with Me109s over Tunbridge Wells, aircraft crashing into Kingswood, Sanderstead, Surrey. Booth baled out low and his parachute caught fire before he hit the ground. Severely injured he eventually died from his wounds on 7 July 1941. He was 20 and came from Sydenham, being buried in Crystal Palace District Cemetery. He had joined the VR in May 1939, and 85 on 15 July 1940.

Victories:	29 Aug	Me109	Destroyed
	30 Aug	Me110	Damaged
	31 Aug	Me110	Probable

14.15   F/O P P Woods-Scawen DFC RAFVR
         85 Sqn
         Hurricane P3150

Shot down by Me109 near Kenley. Baled out but parachute failed; body found on the 6th in the grounds of The Ivies, Kenley Lane. Born in Karachi, India, he lived in South Farnborough, Hampshire from 1924. He was 24 and is buried in St Mary's Churchyard, Caterham-on-the-Hill, Surrey. His elder brother was killed on 2 September (see below, page 81). Son of Philip N & Mrs Kathleen F Woods-Scawen of Farnborough, Hampshire. DFC 25 June 1940. Joined the RAF in October 1937 and then 85 in August 1938. Went to France with this unit in September 1939.

Victories:	10 May	Hs126	Destroyed
	10 May	sh/Ju88	Destroyed
	11 May	sh/Do17	Destroyed
	17 May	Me109	Destroyed
	19 May	Me109	Destroyed
	19 May	Me109	Probable
	19 May	Me109	Destroyed
	19 May	Me109	Destroyed
	29 Jul	Do17	Probable
	26 Aug	Me109	Probable
	26 Aug	½ Do17	Destroyed
	28 Aug	Me109	Destroyed
	30 Aug	Me109	Destroyed
	31 Aug	Me109	Destroyed
	31 Aug	Me109	Destroyed
	31 Aug	Me109	Destroyed

14.15   Sgt J H M Ellis RAFVR
              85 Sqn
              Hurricane P2673

Shot down by Me109 near Kenley. Originally thought to be missing, the crash site at Chelsfield was identified as his in 1992 and an unknown airman burial at St Mary Cray, Orpington, was re-interred in Brookwood Military Cemetery the following year. He was 23, only son of Frederick J & Mrs Ethel M Ellis of Newnham, Cambridge. Joined the VR in September 1938 and was called to full time service exactly one year later. Posted to 85 on 24 May 1940. On 28 August he was shot up over the Channel but glided to the English coast on fire before baling out.

Victories:	6 Aug	½ Do17	Destroyed
	18 Aug	Me109	Destroyed
	18 Aug	Me110	Damaged
	26 Aug	Do17	Destroyed

Monday, 2 September

12.50   Sgt W L Dymond DFM RAF (pictured fourth from left)
              111 Sqn
              Hurricane P3875

Shot down by Me109 over the Thames Estuary. Family in Ruislip, Middlesex and he was 23. No known grave. Son of Thomas & Mrs K Dymond, and husband to Joan M Dymond. Joined the RAF in 1935 and sent to 111 Squadron in August 1936. DFM gazetted 6 September.

Victories:

10 Apr	sh/He111	Destroyed
18 May	Do17	Destroyed
18 May	Do17	Destroyed
31 May	He111	Destroyed
31 May	He111	Destroyed
11 Jun	Me109	Destroyed
13 Aug	Do17	Destroyed
13 Aug	Do17	Damaged
15 Aug	Do17	Destroyed
15 Aug	Do17	Probable
15 Aug	Me110	Destroyed
15 Aug	Me110	Damaged
15 Aug	Me110	Damaged
16 Aug	Do17	Damaged
18 Aug	Do17	Destroyed
18 Aug	Do17	Damaged
24 Aug	He111	Destroyed
30 Aug	Me110	Damaged

13.30   P/O C A Woods-Scawen DFC RAF
43 Sqn
Hurricane V7420

Aircraft set on fire by Me109 over east Kent. Attempted to land at Fryland, near Ivychurch but then baled out, unfortunately too low and he was killed. Also born in Karachi, like his brother, who had been reported missing the previous day (see page 79), he had been brought up in South Farnborough. He was 22 and is buried in Folkestone New Cemetery, Kent. DFC gazetted 6 September 1940. Joined the RAF in March 1938 and 43 Squadron in December 1939.

Victories:

1 Jun	Me109	Probable
7 Jun	Me109	Destroyed
8 Aug	Me110	Destroyed
8 Aug	Ju87	Probable
8 Aug	Ju87	Probable
8 Aug	Ju87	Probable
12 Aug	He111	Damaged
13 Aug	Ju88	Destroyed
13 Aug	Ju88	Destroyed
15 Aug	He111	Destroyed
16 Aug	Ju87	Destroyed
16 Aug	Ju87	Destroyed
30 Aug	Me109	Destroyed

16.30   F/O A T Rose-Price RAF
          501 Sqn
          Hurricane L1578

Missing from combat over Dungeness. Born in Conception, Chile, the son of Brigadier Thomas C Rose-Price & Mrs A Price. He was 25 years old. No known grave. Joined the RAF in 1937. Posted to 501 on 2 September, he was shot down that afternoon. Brother of Dennis Price, the well-known actor.

Tuesday, 3 September

10.35   Sgt G H Edworthy RAF
          46 Sqn
          Hurricane P3064

Failed to return from combat over Essex coast and is thought to have crashed into Redwood Creek, River Crouch. Came from Teignmouth, Devon, was aged 25, and has no known grave. Son of Henry & Mrs Edith M Edworthy of Teignmouth, Devon. Joined the RAF as an apprentice, graduating as a fitter/aero engines in August 1933. His first postings were to the Middle East and Africa. Selected for pilot training in early 1940. Was with 46 Squadron in May 1940 after being with 263 Squadron in Norway.

10.45   P/O C R Bonseigneur RAF
          257 Sqn
          Hurricane P3518

Shot down by fighters over Ingatestone, falling at Lodge Farm, Galleywood, Essex. Baled out but fell dead. Canadian from Gull Lake, Saskatchewan. Aged 22 he is buried in Saffron Walden Cemetery, Essex. Was in the Royal Canadian Signals in September 1937 until June 1939. In October he joined the RAF, going to 257 on 17 May 1940.

Victories: 19 Jul   sh/Do17   Destroyed

10.55   F/O D H W Hanson RAF (pictured overleaf, furthest on left)
          17 Sqn
          Hurricane R4174

Aircraft damaged during combat crashing at Blockhouse Farm, Foulness. Hanson baled out at 100 feet but did not survive. He was 22 and is buried in All Saints Churchyard, Mappleton, Yorkshire. Son of Colonel Harry E Hanson DSO TD & Mrs Ivy A Hanson of Rolston, Hornsea, Essex. He entered Cranwell in September

1936, graduating two years later. Posted to 17 Squadron from 29 Squadron on 23 May 1940.

Victories:

25 May	sh/Do17	Destroyed
25 May	Me109	Probable
26 May	Me109	Probable
3 Jun	Ju87	Damaged
12 Jul	Do17	Destroyed
11 Aug	Me110	Probable
25 Aug	Me109	Probable
3 Sep	Do17	Destroyed

11.15   P/O D W Hogg RAFVR
Sgt E Powell RAF (safe)
25 Sqn
Blenheim L1512

Shot down and crashed near Greensted Green, north-east of Braintree, Essex. Powell baled out. Hogg was 23 years of age and was buried in Eastwood Cemetery, Glasgow. Son of Thomas & Mrs Helen Hogg of Thornliebank, Glasgow. He had joined the RAF on 1 February 1940 with a direct entry commission. He went to 25 on the 11th. Powell was killed in a flying accident on 21 November 1940, the aircraft in which he was flying crashing into the sea. He has no known grave.

11.30   P/O R H Shaw RAFVR
1 Sqn
Hurricane P3782

Crashed at Parkhouse Farm, Chart Sutton, south of Maidstone, cause not known. Officially he is still listed as missing although it has since been established that his remains were buried in Sittingbourne Cemetery though not formally established. He came from Astley Bridge, Bolton and was 24. Joined the VR in October 1937 and 1 Squadron in France on 11 March 1940. He had been shot up by RAF fighters on 1 August, but survived a forced-landing at RAF Tangmere.

11.30   F/L H B L Hillcoat AAF
             1 Sqn
             Hurricane P3044

Missing from patrol. From Bromsgrove, Worcestershire, he was 23 and has no known grave. Son of Henry & Mrs Edith Hillcoat of Bromsgrove, Worcestershire. Joined AAF in 1938. Joined the squadron in France on 10 May 1940. Joined the AAF in 1938 and was posted to 1 Squadron while it was in France on 10 May.

Victories:	4 Jun	He111	Destroyed
	18 Aug	sh/Do17	Destroyed
	1 Sep	Me109	Destroyed
	2 Sep	Me109	Probable

Wednesday, 4 September

09.15   F/L D C Bruce RAF (pictured second from right)
             111 Sqn
             Hurricane R4172

Shot down by Me109 over the Channel off Folkestone. From London, he was 22 and has no known grave. Son of Frederick T & Mrs Ethel Bruce of Kilburn, London. Joined the RAF in 1937, and 111 in February 1938. It is believed he was recommended for the DFC on12 June 1940 but it was not promulgated before his death.

Victories:	8 Apr	½ He111	Probable
	18 May	Me109	Destroyed
	2 Jun	He111	Probable
	2 Jun	Me109	Damaged
	2 Jun	Hs126	Probable
	6 Jun	Me109	Destroyed
	6 Jun	Hs126	Probable
	11 Jun	Me109	Destroyed
	11 Jun	Me109	Destroyed
	11 Jun	Do17	Destroyed
	25 Aug	Me110	Destroyed
	2 Sep	½ He111	Destroyed
	2 Sep	Me110	Damaged

09.15   P/O J Macinski RAF
             111 Sqn
             Hurricane Z2309

Lost over the Channel off Folkestone. Polish pilot aged 24. He has no known grave. In the Polish Air Force pre-war, he escaped to England, being commissioned into the RAF in January 1940. Posted to 111 on 31 August.

10.00   Sgt A D Smith RAF
             66 Sqn
             Spitfire N3048

Shot down over Ashford. Baled out seriously wounded and admitted to No.7 Casualty Clearing Station, Benenden but died on the 6th. He was 22 and is buried in St Luke's churchyard, Whyteleafe, Surrey. Joined the RAF in January 1936 and was posted to 66 in early July 1940.

Victories:	30 Aug	sh/Do17	Destroyed

10.00   F/O A A G Trueman RAF
             253 Sqn
             Hurricane V6638

Shot down in combat over Kenley and crashed in Tudor Close, Banstead, Surrey. A Canadian from Sackville, New Brunswick, he was 26 years old and was buried in St

Luke's Churchyard, Whyteleafe. Son of George & Mrs Agnes Trueman, husband to Mrs Ethel M Trueman of Lincoln. Joined the RAF in March 1938 and became a bomber pilot, flying with 144 Squadron by May 1940. Volunteered to fly fighters and posted to 253 on 20 July. [Insert Pic 2252]

Victories: 2 Sep Me109 Damaged

13.15 F/O R P Plummer RAF
46 Sqn
Hurricane P3052

Shot down by fighters and baled out badly burned about the legs, hands and face. Taken to Southend Municipal Hospital, Rochford Hospital, then transferred to St Luke's Hospital, Bradford, but died of his injuries on the 14th. From Haywards Heath, he was 28, and is buried in Western Road Cemetery, Haywards Heath. Son of George & Beatrice E Plummer of Haywards Heath, Sussex. A former civil servant he had joined the RAF 'F' Class Reserve in August 1936 and the RAF in April 1939. He was posted to 46 in February 1940 and possibly went to Norway with it in May.

13.30 F/O J W Cutts RAF
222 Sqn
Spitfire X4278

Shot down by Me109 over Maidstone, crashing at Amberfield Farm, Chart Sutton. His body was never found, so has no known grave. He came from Felpham, Sussex, aged 20, son of Thomas W & Mrs Daisy J Cutts of Felpham, Sussex. Saw action in July before moving South to Hornchurch on 29 August. Had joined the RAF in April 1938 and was sent to 222 in July 1940.

Victories: 30 Aug sh/He111 Destroyed

13.35 Sgt J W Ramshaw RAFVR
222 Sqn
Spitfire K9962

Shot down by Me109 and crashed at Mockbegger, Collier Street, near Yalding. Ramshaw was badly injured and died before reaching hospital. From Beverley, Yorkshire, aged 24, he is buried in Queensgate Cemetery, Beverley. Son of Harry & Mrs R Ramshaw from Beverley, Yorkshire. He had taken private flying lessons pre-war and joined the VR in April 1937. Once war came he went to 222 on 6 May 1940.

13.40 Sgt J Wright RAF
79 Sqn
Hurricane P3676

Aircraft badly damaged by Me110 over Biggin Hill and crashed at Surbiton. Died of his injuries on the 5th. He was 24 and is buried in New Kilpatrick Cemetery Dumbartonshire. Son of Robert & Mrs Agnes Wright of Kessington, Bearsden, Glasgow. Joining the RAF as an aircraft hand in August 1935, he had applied for pilot training and eventually reached 79 Squadron on 6 July 1940.

Victories: 9 Aug   sh/He111   Destroyed

? Sgt J K Barker RAF
152 Sqn
Spitfire R6909

Shot down by return fire from Do17, twenty-five miles south of Bognor. Baled out but not rescued. Body later washed up on French coast and was buried at Étaples Military Cemetery. He was the 23-year-old son of William R & Mrs Elsie M Barker of Heswell, Cheshire. He had been an apprentice from January 1933, passing out as a wireless operator in December 1935. Applied for pilot training, and having attained that goal went to 152 Squadron as the Battle began.

Victories: 18 Aug   Ju87   Destroyed
25 Aug   Me109   Destroyed

21.30 F/O D K C O'Malley RAFVR
Sgt L A W Rasmussen RNZAF (pictured)
264 Sqn
Defiant N1628

Crashed on take-off in order to intercept an enemy aircraft. O'Malley was 29 years old, son of Barrett L A & Mrs Lorna O'Malley, and husband to Rachel M G O'Malley of Henley-on-Thames, Oxon. He had achieved a BA at Oxford, and was also in the University's Air Squadron. He became a barrister and joined the VR in 1938. Joined 264 in July 1940. Rasmussen was only 18 and had just 19 hours experience as a gunner, but had already served in the NZ territorials in his Auckland home town. Joined the air force and sailed for England in April 1940; posted to 264 on 29 August. Son of Frederick W & Mrs Annie S Rasmussen of Auckland. Both men are buried in the station cemetery at Kirton-in-Lindsey.

Non-operational loss

?   P/O R Ambrose RAFVR
          151 Sqn
          Hurricane V7406

While taking off on a ferry flight to Digby, he crashed into a crane at Stapleford and burned out. He had been in the University Air Squadron while at the London University and was commissioned into the RAFVR in June 1939. Posted to 25 Squadron on 18 August 1940 he moved to 151 on the 26th. He was 21, son of Ivor A & Mrs Laura K Ambrose of Esher, Surrey. He is buried in Epping Cemetery.

Thursday, 5 September

10.00   F/L F W Rushmer AAF (pictured on the left)
          603 Sqn
          Spitfire X4261

Missing after combat over Biggin Hill and may have crashed at Smarden. From Sisland, Norfolk, he was 30 years old, and originally buried as an 'unknown airman' but following extensive investigation his resting place has been confirmed as being in All Saints Churchyard, Staplehurst, Kent. Son of Henry & Mrs Annie J Rushmer of Thurlton, Haddiscoe, Norwich, Norfolk. He received a mention in despatches. He had been slightly wounded on 29 August. Rushmer had joined 603 and the AAF in 1934, and by the time war began he was a section leader.

Victories: 30 Jul   sh/He111   Destroyed

10.15   S/L P C Pinkham AFC RAF
          19 Sqn
          Spitfire P9422

Shot down by Me109 over Thames Estuary, crashing in Whitehorse Wood, Birling, Kent. From Wembley, Middlesex, he was 25 and is buried in St Andrew's Churchyard, Kingsbury, Middlesex. Son of Lieutenant Philip I Pinkham RNVR & Mrs Nora Pinkham of Wembley, Middlesex. His AFC was awarded in July 1940 for his instructing abilities between 1938 and 1940. He had joined the RAF in April 1935 and after a spell with 17 Squadron from February 1936 had been with the Meteorological Flight at RAF Mildenhall from August 1937. A post at 11 Group HQ in 1938, then an instructor at the Air Fighting school at Sutton Bridge, he then became an instructor with 11 Group Pilot Pool in 1939, taking command of this unit in January 1940. Took command of 19 Squadron in June.

14.25 P/O D C Winter RAF
72 Sqn
Spitfire X4013

Shot down by Me109 over Eltham. Baled out too low and was killed. From South Shields, Tyneside, he was 26 and is buried in Harton Cemetery, in his home town. Son of Douglas C & Mrs Margaret Winter of South Shields, and husband to Mrs Marjorie Winter. He had been in the athletics team in the 1932 King's Cup, and had been awarded two shooting medals at Bisley. He had joined the RAF in 1929 as an apprentice fitter and had been in the Middle East prior to pilot training. He was posted to 72 on 1 April 1940 and commissioned.

Victories:	2 Jun	Ju87	Destroyed
	29 Jun	sh/Do17	Destroyed
	15 Aug	Me110	Destroyed
	15 Aug	Me110	Destroyed
	1 Sep	Me109	Destroyed

14.25 Sgt M Gray RAFVR
72 Sqn
Spitfire N3093

Shot down over Eltham by Me109. He was 20 years old from Heworth, Yorkshire, and is buried in Fulford Cemetery, North Yorkshire. Son of George W & Mrs Emily Gray of Heworth, York. He had joined the VR in the summer of 1938 and when trained was posted to 72 Squadron in June 1940.

15.25 F/L J T Webster DFC RAF
41 Sqn
Spitfire R6635

Collided with his CO's Spitfire P9428 during attack on enemy aircraft over the Thames Estuary. Crashed at Markham Chase School, Laindon. Webster baled out but landed dead. He was from Liverpool, aged 24, and is buried in Darlington Cemetery. Educated at Liverpool College. Joined the RAF in August 1935 and after a year with 80 Squadron – March 1937 to April 1938 – moved to 41 Squadron. Awarded the DFC, gazetted on 30 August.

Victories:	17 Dec '39	He115	Probable
	31 May	Me109	Destroyed
	31 May	½ He111	Destroyed
	1 Jun	Do17	Destroyed
	1 Jun	Do17	Probable

19/20 Jun	He111	Destroyed
27 Jul	Me109	Destroyed
28 Jul	Me109	Damaged
28 Jul	Me109	Destroyed
29 Jul	Me109	Destroyed
29 Jul	Ju87	Damaged
5 Aug	He111	Damaged
8 Aug	½ Me109	Destroyed
8 Aug	Me109	Destroyed
8 Aug	Me109	Destroyed
8 Aug	Me109	Destroyed
5 Sep	Me109	Destroyed
5 Sep	Me109	Destroyed

15.25   S/L H R L Hood (DFC)
41 Sqn
Spitfire P9428

Collided with Spitfire R6635 in combat over Thames Estuary. Spitfire disintegrated over Wickford and fell into the sea. He was 32 years old and has no known grave. His DFC citation appeared in the London Gazette 27 May 1941 wef 11 August 1940. He was the younger son of the late John L B Hood & Mrs Helene M Hood, who remarried and went to live in South Africa. Born in Paddington, London, he became a Cranwell Cadet in 1927-29. Took command of 41 Squadron in April 1940. He was one of the oldest fighter pilots to take part in the Battle.

Victories:	29 Jul	Me109	Destroyed
	29 Jul	Ju87	Destroyed
	5 Sep	Do17	Damaged

15.30   Sgt A L McNay RAFVR (pictured on left)
73 Sqn
Hurricane P3224

Fell in combat over Burnham and crashed at North Fambridge, Essex. He came from Shawlands Cross, Glasgow but his body was never found, therefore he has no known grave. He was 22 years old, son of John & Mrs Williamena McNay. Was with the Squadron in France in June 1940. He had joined the VR in May 1938 and, completing his training, was posted to 73 Squadron in June 1940.

Victories:	15 Aug	Ju88	Destroyed
	15 Aug	Ju88	Destroyed

16.00   F/O P J C King RAF
66 Sqn
Spitfire N3060

Shot down by Me109 over Medway. Baled out but parachute failed to open. From Farnborough, Warwickshire, he was 19, and is buried in St Botolph's Churchyard in his home town. He was the son of Colonel Harold J King (Royal Artillery) & Mrs Elsie M King. Joined the RAF in September 1938 and 66 in July 1940.

Victories: 4 Sep   Me109   Destroyed

Friday, 6 September

09.00   P/O H C Adams RAFVR
501 Sqn
Hurricane V6612

Shot down over Ashford, Kent and crashed at Clavertye, Eltham. He was from Oxted, Surrey and was 22. He is buried in St Peter's Churchyard, Tandridge, Surrey. Son of John C & Mrs Grace Adams of Chaddleworth, Berkshire. Joined the VR in January 1938 and 501 on 17 July 1940.

Victories: 2 Sep   Me109   Destroyed

09.00   Sgt O V Houghton RAFVR
501 Sqn
Hurricane V6646

Shot down over Ashford, Kent, crashing into Long Beech Wood, Charing. He came from Failshill, Coventry, aged 19, and is buried at All Saints Churchyard extension, Charing, Kent. Son of Sidney & Mrs Alice L Houghton of Coventry. Joined the Civil Air Guard in 1938 and the RAFVR in March 1939, 615 Squadron in June 1940, 32 Squadron in July and then to 501 on 27 August.

09.00   Sgt G W Pearson RAFVR
501 Sqn
Hurricane P3516

Missing from combat over Ashford. Crashed at Cowless Farm, near Kempton Manor, Hothfield. Originally buried as an 'unknown' airman in St Stephen's Churchyard, Lympne, Kent but in 1982 his sister finally established it was her brother's grave and a correctly-named headstone was erected there. He was 21, the son of Vivian W & Mrs Freida M Pearson of East End, Oxfordshire. Joined the VR in December 1938 and 501 in late August 1940.

09.10   P/O W H G Gordon RAF
234 Sqn
Spitfire X4036

Shot down by Me109, crashing at Howbourne Farm, Hadlow Down. From Aberdeen, he was 20 years old and is buried in Mortlach Parish Churchyard, Banff. Son of Major William Gordon DSO MC & Mrs Maggie A Pearson of Dufftown, Scotland. He had joined the RAF in March 1939 and was with 234 in early July 1940.

Victories: 24 Aug   Me109   Destroyed

09.15   F/L W P Cambridge RAF
253 Sqn
Hurricane P3032

Baled out during patrol on 6 September due to engine trouble. Parachute failed and aircraft crashed at Kingsnorth. Buried at Henley Road Cemetery, Reading, Berks. Born in India in 1912, son of Sidney J and Agnes H Cambridge, of Caversham, Berks. Joined RAF in 1936 and served with 253 Squadron from late October 1939. He had been made acting CO on 30 August 1940.

Victories: 30 Aug   Me110   Destroyed
4 Sep   Me110   Destroyed

09.30   P/O C R Davis DFC BA AAF
601 Sqn
Hurricane P3363

Shot down by Me109, crashed at Matfield, Brenchley, near Tunbridge Wells. Davis was an American, but born in South Africa, and came to England aged 13. He was 29 when killed and is buried in Storrington, Sussex. He was married to the sister of his CO, Sir Archibald Hope. Became a BA (Cantab) and had a BA from McGill University, Montreal, Canada. A former mining engineer he was the son of Carl R & Mrs Clara M Davis and married to Katherine A Davis of Chelsea, London. His DFC was awarded on 30 August. He had joined the AAF and 601 Squadron in 1936. He had been part of a small force of Blenheims of 601 that had attacked the German seaplane base at Borkum, on 27 November 1939.

Victories: 11 Jul   Me110   Destroyed
26 Jul   Me109   Damaged

11 Aug	Me110	Probable
11 Aug	Me110	Probable
11 Aug	Me110	Damaged
13 Aug	Ju88	Damaged
13 Aug	½ Ju88	Probable
13 Aug	Me110	Destroyed
13 Aug	Me110	Destroyed
13 Aug	Me110	Destroyed
13 Aug	Me110	Damaged
13 Aug	Me110	Probable
15 Aug	Ju88	Destroyed
16 Aug	Ju87	Destroyed
18 Aug	Ju87	Destroyed
18 Aug	½ Ju87	Destroyed
18 Aug	Me109	Destroyed
31 Aug	Me110	Probable
4 Sep	Me110	Destroyed

09.30   F/L W H Rhodes-Moorhouse DFC AAF
               601 Sqn
               Hurricane P8818

Shot down by Me109 over Tunbridge Wells, crashing near High Brooms Viaduct, Southborough. His parents were Captain William B & Mrs Linda B Rhodes-Moorhouse, of Parnham House. His father had won the Victoria Cross in World War One. He was born in Brompton Square, Kensington, London, and was 26 when he was killed. He was buried in a private family home cemetery, at Parnham, Beaminster, Dorset. He was educated at Eton and competed in the Winter Games of 1937/38 in skiing. His DFC was awarded on 30 July 1940. He had joined the AAF and 601 in 1937, having already gained his private pilot licence when he was aged 17. His mother was also a qualified pilot. Young William married Amelia Demetriadi, daughter of Sir Stephen Demetriadi KBE in 1936, whose brother Richard Demetriadi, also of 601 Squadron, had been killed in action on 11 August.

Victories:	18 May	He111	Destroyed
	22 May	Me109	Destroyed
	7 Jul	sh/Do17	Destroyed
	11 Jul	sh/Do17	Destroyed
	16 Jul	sh/Ju88	Destroyed
	16 Jul	Ju88	Destroyed
	11 Aug	Me109	Probable
	11 Aug	Me109	Probable

18 Aug	Me109	Destroyed
30 Aug	¼ He111	Destroyed
31 Aug	Me109	Probable
31 Aug	Me109	Probable
4 Sep	Do17	Destroyed

Saturday, 7 September

London became the Germans' priority from this date. Because Churchill had ordered retaliatory raids on Berlin, Hitler's fury meant that hostilities against the British people became paramount in his mind. It came at a time when attacks on RAF fighter airfields was starting to have an effect, and had these continued, matters might have turned out very differently. On the logistics side, the Luftwaffe had suffered heavily while engaged on these attacks, and its bomber squadrons started to fly night-raids in an effort to stem these losses.

This became the beginning of the Third Phase of the Battle. It was a sobering thought for pilots of 605 Squadron, ordered down from the north to its new base at RAF Croydon. As they landed at around 7.30 pm, they could see lots of smoke rising from the conurbation that was nearby London. As one pilot remarked: 'My God, we really are in the thick of it; we're really up against it.'

14.30 P/O W Krepski RAF
54 Sqn
Spitfire R6901

Missing from operational sortie over Flamborough Head area and is believed to have crashed into the sea. Polish pilot, aged 23, he has no known grave. He was in the Polish Air Force pre-war and arrived in England in January 1940. After converting onto Spitfires he was posted to 54 Squadron on 23 August.

16.45 S/L C B Hull DFC RAF (pictured on right)
43 Sqn
Hurricane V6641

Shot down by Me109, south London, crashed at Purley High School grounds. From Shangani, Southern Rhodesia, and later Swaziland, he was 26 when he died. South African Air Force Reserve in 1935 then moved to the RAF, flying with 43 Squadron from August 1936, becoming a flight commander in 1938. In combat in early 1940, he then took part in the Norwegian Expedition, flying Gladiators from a frozen lake in April. His DFC was gazetted on 21 June. Son of William B & Mrs Winifred C Hull of Breyton, Transvaal. He was buried in St Andrew's Churchyard, Tangmere. His older brother Robin died on 1 January 1942, while with the Rand Light Infantry in North Africa.

Victories:	30 Jan	½ He111	Destroyed
	28 Mar	¼ He111	Destroyed
	10 Apr	sh/He111	Destroyed
	24 May	sh/He111	Destroyed
	26 May	He111	Probable
	26 May	Ju52	Destroyed
	26 May	Ju52	Destroyed
	26 May	Ju52	Damaged
	26 May	He111	Damaged
	27 May	Ju87	Destroyed
	4 Sep	Me109	Probable
	4 Sep	Me109	Probable
	6 Sep	Me109	Destroyed
	6 Sep	½ Ju88	Probable

16.45   F/L R C Reynell RAFO
43 Sqn
Hurricane V7257

Shot down by Me109 over Blackheath, baled out wounded but his parachute failed. He was an Australian, aged 28, and buried in Brookwood Cemetery, Surrey. Born in Reynella, South Australia, he came to the UK in 1929, going to Oxford University. Commissioned into the RAFO in 1931, he later became a test pilot at Farnborough (AFRAeS). His father, Lieutenant-Colonel C Reynell, Australian Light Horse, was killed in France in August 1915. His mother was May Reynell of Reynella, South Australia. He was married to Enid M Reynell, West End, near Woking, Surrey. Attached to 43 Squadron for operational experience.

Victories:	2 Sep	Me109	Destroyed

17.00   F/L R E Lovett DFC RAF (pictured middle)
73 Sqn
Hurricane P3234

Shot down in combat, crashed on Fritze Farm, near Billericay, Essex. Born Hendon, north London, he was 26 and is buried in Hendon Cemetery. Son of Reginald & Mrs Lily Lovett of Golders Green, North London. Joined the RAF in November 1935, his first unit was 66 Squadron from August 1936, before becoming a flight commander with 73 as war started. Flew with 73 in France and was awarded the DFC, gazetted 16 July 1940.

Victories:	22 Mar	Me109	Destroyed
	26 Mar	Do17	Damaged
	21 Apr	Me110	Destroyed
	10 May	½ EA	Damaged
	15 Aug	Ju88	Destroyed
	15 Aug	Ju88	Probable

17.00   P/O J Benzie RAF
242 Sqn
Hurricane P2962

Failed to return after combat above the Thames Estuary. Canadian, came from Winnipeg and was 25 when he died. Although officially he has no known grave, remains that are thought to be his are in Brookwood Cemetery, as an 'Unknown Pilot'. Son of John & Mrs Agnes Benzie of Winnipeg, Canada, he had served in the Princess Patricia's Canadian Light Infantry prior to joining the RAF shortly before the war. Posted to 242 in January 1940. Had seen action in France, being wounded on 23 May by Me109 attack and evacuated to England. He arrived back on the Squadron on 11 July.

17.00   P/O R D S Fleming RAFVR
249 Sqn
Hurricane R4114

Shot down in combat over Maidstone and crashed at Hollingbourne. This 20-year-old was cremated at Golders Green Crematorium. Son of Robert S & Mrs Eleanor Fleming of Hampstead, North London, joined the Squadron on 23 June 1940. He had been a member of the University Air Squadron while at London University. Joined the VR in July 1939 and was posted to 249 on 23 June 1940.

17.00   F/O K V Wendel RAF (pictured left)
504 Sqn
Hurricane L1615

Shot down over the Thames Estuary and crashed near Graveney, Faversham. Wendel was badly burned and died of his injuries. A New Zealander from Auckland, aged 24, he was buried in Faversham Cemetery, Kent. Son of Charles V & Mrs Christina M Wendel, of Auckland, NZ. He had been a member and pupil of the Auckland Flying Corps. Accepted for RAF training in May 1937 he came to England that December. Once trained he was a staff pilot at No.1 Electrical & Wireless School at RAFCranwell. Posted to 504 on 23 January 1940, saw action in France. After being based in Scotland in May, the Squadron flew south on 5 September. He was killed on its first operational sortie from Hendon.

17.30   F/O W H Coverley RAFO
         602 Sqn
         Spitfire N3198

Shot down over Biggin Hill area, crashing in flames at Fosters Farm, near Tonbridge. He baled out, badly burned, and later died of his injuries, although his body was not located until the 16th. He was 23 and was buried in Dean Road Cemetery, Scarborough. Son of Thomas C & Mrs Mary E Coverley of Lowdham, Nottinghamshire. Commissioned with the RAFO in December 1936, he was posted to 602 in June 1940. Shot down and baled out on 25 August.

Victories: 7 Jul   sh/Ju88   Destroyed

17.30   P/O H W Moody RAFVR
         602 Sqn
         Spitfire X4256

Missing from fight over Biggin Hill area. He was 30 years old and has no known grave. He had joined the VR in mid-1937, joined 602 as a sergeant-pilot in March 1940 and was commissioned in June. He had been shot down on 19 August during an attack on a Ju88, and baled out with slight burns to his hands.

Victories: 16 Aug   Me110   Destroyed
             18 Aug   Ju87   Destroyed
             4 Sep   Do17   Destroyed

17.30   F/L H R A Beresford RAF
         257 Sqn
         Hurricane P3049

Shot down over the Thames Estuary. Crashed at Elmley, Sheppey. Body not recovered but was found in a 1979 excavation of the crash-site. Buried at Brookwood Cemetery. From Ampthill, Bedfordshire, he was aged 24 and the son of the Rector of Hoby, Leicestershire. Joined the RAF in 1935 and flew with 3 Squadron at Port Sudan in 1936. Some time after returning to the UK he became a flight commander with 257 Squadron.

Victories: 18 Aug   sh/He111   Destroyed
               31 Aug   Me110   Destroyed

17.30   F/O L R G Mitchell RAF
            257 Sqn
            Hurricane V7254

Shot down in combat over Thames Estuary. From Keith, Banffshire, he has no known grave. Aged 24, the son of Robert G & Mrs Elizabeth S Mitchell. A member of the RAFO in August 1937 he received a short service commission in the RAF and was with 85 Squadron in July 1938. Posted to 611 Squadron as the war started he moved to 257 on 17 May 1940.

Victories: 19 Jul   sh/Do17   Destroyed
               31 Aug   Me110   Destroyed

18.25   S/L J S O'Brien DFC RAF
            234 Sqn
            Spitfire P9466

Shot down in combat over St Mary Cray, crashing near Biggin Hill. He was 28 and is buried in St Mary Cray Cemetery, Orpington, Kent. Was a merchant navy cadet before joining the RAF in 1934. When war began he was flying Blenheim night-fighters with 23 Squadron. He and a Spitfire pilot shot down a night raider on 18/19 June although both aircraft were hit by return fire. Only O'Brien survived, but he received a mention in despatches. Joined 92 Squadron as a supernumerary on 1 July then took command of 234 on 17 August, having been awarded the DFC. He was a married man. His father, a major, was killed in WW1.

Victories: 18/19 Jun   He111   Destroyed
               21 Aug   sh/Ju88   Destroyed
               24 Aug   Me109   Destroyed
               6 Sep   Me109   Destroyed
               6 Sep   Me109   Destroyed

18.25   F/L P C Hughes DFC RAF
234 Sqn
Spitfire X4009

Collided with a Do17 near Folkestone, and crashed at Darks
Farm, Bessels Green, Sevenoaks, Kent. Born in Cooma, New
South Wales, Australia, he is buried in St James' Churchyard,
Sutton, Hull. He was ten days short of his 23rd birthday. He
entered the RAAF as a cadet in 1936, came to England the
following year to join the RAF and after a brief spell with 64
Squadron, moved to 234 at the end of October 1939. Awarded
the DFC, gazetted on 22 October 1940. Son of Peterson C &
Mrs C C Hughes, husband of Kathleen A Hughes of Hull, Humberside.

Victories:	8 Jul	sh/Ju88	Destroyed
	27 Jul	sh/Ju88	Probable
	28 Jul	sh/Ju88	Destroyed
	15 Aug	Me110	Destroyed
	15 Aug	½ Me110	Destroyed
	16 Aug	Me109	Destroyed
	16 Aug	Me109	Destroyed
	18 Aug	Me109	Destroyed
	18 Aug	Me109	Destroyed
	26 Aug	Me109	Destroyed
	26 Aug	Me109	Destroyed
	4 Sep	Me109	Destroyed
	4 Sep	Me109	Destroyed
	4 Sep	Me109	Destroyed
	5 Sep	Me109	Destroyed
	5 Sep	Me109	Destroyed
	6 Sep	Me109	Destroyed
	6 Sep	Me109	Probable
	7 Sep	Do17	Destroyed

Non-operational loss

15.50   Sgt A F C Saunders RAFVR
Sgt J W Davies RAFVR
600 Sqn
Blenheim L6684

During a landing approach one engine failed causing the machine to turn over
and crash onto its back from 200 feet, at Rainham in Essex. Both men were killed
instantly. Saunders was 19, son of Albert B & Mrs Eliza A Saunders of Clapham,
south London. He is buried in Wandsworth Cemetery at Earlsfield. Davies was 22,

son of Oswald B & Mrs Winifred M A Davies of Leeds. He is buried in St John's Churchyard, Roundhay, Leeds.

12.05   F/O D J Sanders RAF
          54 Sqn
          Spitfire P9560

Crashed while at a low altitude during a training flight, cause not known. He was the 21-year-old son of Richard J & Mrs Amy Sanders of Quinton, Birmingham, and is buried in Catterick Cemetery. Commissioned into the RAF in January 1939.

Sunday, 8 September

12.15   F/O W J M Scott RAFVR
          41 Sqn
          Spitfire R6756

Fell in flames during patrol off Dover, probably shot down by Me109. From Dundee, he was 25 and is buried in Dundee Western Cemetery. Went to Corpus Christi College, Cambridge, where he joined the University Air Squadron while studying to become a BA (Cantab). Commissioned into the RAFO in March 1937 he relinquished this to become a VR officer on 1 January 1938. Joined 41 Squadron in July 1940. Son of William M & Mrs Katherine E Scott of South Kensington, London.

Victories: 7 Sep   Me109   Destroyed

12.30   Sub-Lt J C Carpenter RN
          46 Sqn
          Hurricane P3201

Shot down during attack on enemy aircraft over Sheppey and crashed at Bearsted, Maidstone. Baled out but died. He was 21. His body was taken to his family at Llanfaethlu, Angelsey, and was later buried at sea. Son of Major Frederick N & Mrs Ida M Carpenter of Llanfaethlu. Fleet Air Arm in July 1939, attached to the RAF in June 1940, and 46 Squadron on 23 July.

Victories: 3 Sep   Me110   Destroyed
          5 Sep   Me109   Destroyed

Monday, 9 September

17.30   P/O G M Forrester RAFVR
605 Sqn
Hurricane L2059

Hit by return fire from He111s of KG53 over Farnborough, then collided with a Heinkel losing his starboard wing, north of Alton, falling at Southfield Farm. From Newcastle, he was 26 and is buried at Odiham Cemetery, Hampshire. Son of James & Mrs Elsie Forrester of Upper Bassett, and husband to Frances E Forrester. A keen rower and rugby player he had joined the VR in the spring of 1938, and was posted to 605 on 3 August 1940. His younger brother Michael became Major-General Forrester CB CBE DSO & Bar, MC & Bar.

17.30   P/O S B Parnall AAF
607 Sqn
Hurricane P3574

Shot down in combat over Mayfield and crashed on Lime Tree Farm, Goudhurst. From Walthamstow, Essex, he was 30 and was cremated at Golders Green Crematorium, Hendon. His elder brother, S/L J B Parnall, CO of 504 Squadron, was killed in action in France on 14 May 1940, shot down by JG26, while his other brother was also in France. Their parents were John B & Mrs Ethel M A Parnall of Walthamstow, Essex. Parnell had joined 607 and the AAF in early 1939, and once war began returned for full time service with 607 who by then were in France.

17.30   P/O G J Drake RAF
607 Sqn
Hurricane P2728

Shot down over Mayfield and crashed at Bockingfold Farm, Goudhurst. Drake was originally placed on the missing list, however his Hurricane was excavated in 1972 and his remains were discovered. He was South African from Huguenot, Cape Province. This 20-year-old was laid to rest at Brookwood Military Cemetery. He had originally tried to join the SAAF but being rejected, made his way to England to join the RAF, which he did in June 1939. Posted to 607 in France on 20 April 1940.

17.35   P/O J D Lenahan RAF
607 Sqn
Hurricane P3117

Shot down in combat over Mayfield, crashed Mount Ephraim, Cranbrook. From Hayes, Middlesex, he was 20 and buried in Cranbrook Cemetery, Kent. Son of John M & Mrs Edith Lenahan of Hayes, Middlesex. Went to 263 Squadron initially, before moving to 607 Squadron on 1 June 1940, having joined the RAF in August 1938.

17.35   F/O J E Boulton RAF
310 Sqn
Hurricane P3888

Collided with another Hurricane during combat over Croydon, then hit a Do17. From Bosham, Sussex, he was 20, and is buried in Bandon Hill Cemetery, Beddington, Surrey. His father was a WW1 veteran who died in a road accident in 1929. Boulton joined the RAF in October 1937 and became a qualified flying instructor by 1938, attached to 310 Squadron on 11 July to help convert Czech pilots onto the Hurricane. He requested operational status, remaining with 310. He later received a posthumous Czech Military Cross.

Victories: 7 Sep   ½ He111   Destroyed

17.45   P/O K M Sclanders RAFVR
242 Sqn
Hurricane P3087

Shot down in combat over Thames Haven, crashing at Marden Park, Caterham. A Canadian from Saskatoon, he was 24 and is buried in St Luke's Churchyard, Whyteleafe, Surrey. He had been taught to fly at the age of 15, finally getting a licence two years later. Taking part in air shows, he would act as a Boy Scout who accidentally started an aircraft engine, taking off to perform aerobatics. He came to England in 1935 in order to join the RAF, but had to resign due to ill-health in 1937. Regaining his health he tried to join in the Russo-Finnish war but as this ended he tried the French, but again he was too late, so sailed across to England and managed to get into the RAFVR. He was posted to 242 on 26 August 1940.

September 1940

Tuesday, 10 September

No operational fatalities

Wednesday, 11 September

11.00 Sgt S Andrew RAFVR (pictured third from right)
46 Sqn
Hurricane P3525

Crashed during patrol, cause not known. From Swanland, Yorkshire, he was 21 years old and is buried in All Saints Churchyard, North Ferriby, Yorkshire. Son of John W & Mrs Amelia Andrew of Swanland. A VR pilot from April 1937 he went to 46 in March 1939. Served in the fight for Norway in April 1940, and was one of the lucky survivors when the carrier Glorious was sunk on 8 June. Was back with 46 as it reformed in late June.

Victories: 8 Sep   Do17   Destroyed

15.30   Sgt W A Peacock AAF
       46 Sqn
       Hurricane V7232

Lost during combat over the Thames Estuary. Aged 20 from Seaton Carew, Durham, he has no known grave. Son of Albert & Mrs Catherine R Peacock of South Bank, Middlesborough, Yorkshire. Joined 608 Squadron AAF in early 1938 and once a pilot was posted to 46 Squadron on 18 July 1940.

Victories: 8 Sep   Me109   Destroyed

16.00   Sgt A Wojcicki PAF
       213 Sqn
       Hurricane V6667

Shot down into the Channel by Me110. Polish pilot aged 26. He has no known grave and his name appears on the Polish Air Force Memorial at Northolt. Came to England and enlisted into the RAF in February 1940, transferring to the PAF on 6 August.

16.00   P/O A W Clarke RAF
       504 Sqn
       Hurricane P3770

Shot down over Kent coast, and crashed south of Rookelands, near Newchurch. From Altrincham, Cheshire, he was 20 at the time of his death. Investigation of the crash site confirmed the aircraft's identity and next of kin decided to leave it undisturbed. On 11 September 1986, a memorial was dedicated here. Son of the late Frank & Lavinia Clarke. Worked for the Air Ministry before joining the RAF in June 1939. Once trained was posted to 504 on 7 April 1940.

16.00   Sgt F E R Shepherd AAF
       611 Sqn
       Spitfire II P7298

Spitfire set on fire during combat over Croydon. Pilot baled out but his parachute caught fire and he was killed. He was 22 and is buried at St Luke's Churchyard, Whyteleafe, Surrey. Son of William H & Mrs Blodwen J Shepherd of Prestatyn, Flintshire, and husband of Mrs Thelma M Shepherd. He had joined the AAF pre-war as an aircraft hand with 611 but responded to a scheme to train such men as pilots. As the war started he completed his training and returned to 611 on 1 September 1940.

16.15   P/O F N Hargreaves RAF
92 Sqn
Spitfire K9793

Missing after combat action over Dungeness. From Manchester he was 21 and has no known grave. Son of James F R & Mrs Annie Hargreaves of Manchester. He joined the RAF in June 1939 and posted to 92 in March 1940. He had to bale out of his Spitfire on 27 August having got himself lost during a night flying exercise.

16.15   F/L D P Hughes DFC RAF
238 Sqn
Hurricane V7240

Missing after engaging Ju88s over Tunbridge Wells. He was not seen again and has no known grave, although a crash site has been under investigation. He was 22, the son of Arthur P & Mrs Mary Hughes of St Anne's-on-the-Sea, Lancashire, and husband of Joan. His DFC was awarded in May 1941, back-dated to 21 August 1940.

He joined the RAF in 1936 and had served with 16 and 53 Squadrons before being posted to 238 as a flight commander in early August 1940.

Victories:	8 Aug	Me110	Destroyed
	11 Aug	Me109	Destroyed
	13 Aug	Do17	Destroyed
	13 Aug	Me109	Probable
	13 Aug	Me110	Destroyed
	13 Aug	Me110	Destroyed

16.15   Sgt S Duszynski
238 Sqn
Hurricane R2682

Failed to return after action against Ju88s pursued over Romney Marsh. Aircraft crashed at Little Scotney Farm, Lydd. Officially noted has having no known grave, some items were found at the crash site some years later, but no human remains. He was 24 years old. He had arrived from Poland, via France, in 1940 and once converted to Hurricanes was posted to 238 Squadron on 2 September.

16.15   F/O A Cebrzynski
303 Sqn
Hurricane V6667

Shot down south of London and crashed at Hitchens Farm, Pembury. Pilot severely injured and died on 19 September. He was 28 and had fought over Poland and France. He was buried in Northwood Cemetery, Middlesex. Had fought in Poland and then in France, with III/1 Dyon. Escaped to France and commanded a flight of three Polish pilots in Groupe de Chasse II/6 flying Bloch 152s. Came to England in July and was posted to 303 on 21 August. Shortly after his death, he was awarded the Krzyż Walecznych (KW) – the Cross of Valor.

Victories:	3 Sep '39	Me110	Destroyed
	6 Sep	sh/Ju87	Destroyed
	6 Sep	Me110	Destroyed
	5 Jun '40	He111	Destroyed
	5 Jun	sh/He111	Destroyed
	15 Jun	sh/Hs126	Destroyed

16.15   Sgt S Wojtowicz
303 Sqn
Hurricane V7242

Shot down by Me109 over south London, crashed on Hogtrough Hill, Westerham. Born Wynich, Poland he was 24. Buried in Northwood Cemetery, Middlesex. Joined PAF in 1936 and flew with the 111 Fighter Wing. Evacuated to Romania he made his way to France, and flew in a Polish formation defending Nantes. Escaped to England and was posted to 303 on 2 August 1940.

Victories:	7 Sep	Do17	Destroyed
	7 Sep	Do17	Destroyed
	11 Sep	Me109	Destroyed
	11 Sep	Me109	Probable

16.20   Sgt M H Sprague RAFVR
602 Sqn
Spitfire N3282

Shot down by Me110 south of Selsey Bill. He came from Richmond, Surrey and was 21. He is buried at Tangmere, having been washed up at Brighton on 10 October. Joined the VR in 1935 while employed as a chartered accountant in his father's firm. Served in the 'F' Reserve Class of the RAF from May 1935, then joined the RAFVR in May 1938. Went to 602 on 18 June 1940. Had already been shot down into the sea on 25 August but had been rescued.

17.30   P/O P C Wickings-Smith RAF (pictured left)
P/O A W V Green RAFVR
Sgt R D H Watts RAFVR (pictured right)
235 Sqn
Blenheim Z5725

Shot down by Me109 during escort mission off Calais. From Bedford, the pilot was 22. Green came from Craigavad, Co. Down and was 21. Watts from Far Colton, Northampton, was 35. They have no known graves. The pilot was the son of Claude T & Mrs Vera F Wickings-Smith. Green was the son of Alexander & Mrs Marjory Green of Craigavad, Co. Down. Watts was the son of Charles & Mrs Alice L Watts of Far Cotton, Northamptonshire.

17.30   F/L F W Flood RAF
P/O N B Shorrocks RAFVR
Sgt B R Sharp RAFVR
235 Sqn
Blenheim L9396

Flood, from Roma, Queensland, Australia, led the escort mission and was shot down by a Me109. He was 25. Shorrocks was 29 and Sharp 27. They have no known graves.

19.00   P/O H D Edwards RAF
92 Sqn
Spitfire P9464

Shot down by Me109, crashing into a wood at Evegate Manor Farm, Smeeth, south-east of Ashford. A Canadian from Winnipeg he was 24. The wreck of his machine was not found until 7 October and his remains were buried in Folkestone New Cemetery (Hawkinge), Kent. Son of John H & Mrs Emily M Edwards. Joined the RAF in January 1939 and 92 in October 1939. Saw action over France and Dunkirk.

Victories:	23 May	Ju88	Destroyed
	23 May	Me109	Probable
	23 May	Me109	Probable
	23 May	Me110	Probable
	24 May	Me109	Probable
	2 Jun	He111	Destroyed
	4 Jul	sh/He111	Destroyed

Thursday, 12 September

?   W/C J S Dewar DSO DFC RAF
Exeter
Hurricane V7306

Failed to arrive at Tangmere on a routine flight from Exeter, and his body was washed ashore at Kingston Gore, Sussex on 30 September. It was thought he had been shot down and strafed while in his parachute. He had been born at Mussoorie, Lahore Province, India and was 33 years old. Buried North Baddesley (St John the Baptist) Churchyard, Hampshire. He was the second son of Douglas Dewar working in India but originally from Camberley, Surrey. Dewar became a Cranwell cadet in 1926 and for a time was attached to the Fleet Air Arm before going to A&AEE in 1938. He was Senior Operations Officer at Thorney Island later in 1938. CO of 87 Squadron November 1939. DSO 20 May and DFC 31 May 1940. He was the most senior RAF pilot to die in the Battle.

Victories:	11 May	½ Do17	Destroyed
	11 Jul	Me110	Destroyed
	11 Jul	Me110	Probable
	11 May	Me110	Destroyed
	13 Aug	½ Ju88	Destroyed
	25 May	Ju88	Destroyed
	25 Aug	Me109	Probable

Friday, 13 September

0.700   Sgt W J Garfield RAFVR (pictured)
Sgt B W Mesner RAFVR
Sgt A Kay RAF
248 Sqn
Blenheim L9451

Failed to return from reconnaissance mission to Norwegian coast. Garfield came from Sutton-in-Ashfield, Nottinghamshire, aged 25, son of Walter S & Mrs Emma M Garfield. He is buried in Mollendal Cemetery, Bergen. Mesner came from Forrest Gate, Essex, aged 29, son of Charles and Adelaide Mesner, and husband to Jessie Mesner. He has no known grave. Kay, who joined the RAF in June 1939, was 24 and also has no known grave.

Garfield, pictured on far left.

Sgt BW Mesner.

Saturday, 14 September

16.05   Sgt J J Brimble RAFVR
           73 Sqn
           Hurricane P2542

Shot down over the Tonbridge area, crashing at Parkhouse Farm, Chart Sutton. From Knowle, Bristol, aged 23, he was originally noted as missing. However, when excavating his aircraft crash site in 1980, his remains were found, and buried in Brookwood Cemetery, that October. Son of William H & Mrs Emily A Brimble. Joined the VR in May 1938 and once fully trained was posted to 73 Squadron in France on 31 May 1940.

16.15   Sgt S Baxter RAF
           222 Sqn
           Spitfire X4275

Badly damaged in combat with Me109s he crashed attempting a landing at Rochford. From Birtley, Co Durham, he was 24 years old. Cremated in Newcastle-upon-Tyne (West Road) Crematorium. Son of Edward R & Mrs Jessie Baxter. Became an aircraft apprentice in January 1933, passing out as a fitter. Remustered as a trainee pilot and, having become one, went to 222 Squadron early in 1940.

Victories: 1 Jun   Me110   Destroyed

16.20   Sgt F Marek
              19 Sqn
              Spitfire R6625

Crashed near Hordon-on-the-Hill, Orsett, possibly caused by oxygen failure, during routine patrol. Born at Ceske Budejovic, Czechoslovakia, he was 27. Buried in Easterbrookend Cemetery, Barking, Essex. He was with 310 Squadron, attached to 19.

18.00   Sgt W B Higgins RAFVR
              253 Sqn
              Hurricane P5184

Shot down by Me109 and crashed on Swanton Farm, Bredger, south of Sittingbourne, Essex. From Hodthorpe, Whitwell, Derbyshire, he was 26. He is buried in St Lawrence's Churchyard, Whitnall. A former school teacher he was the son of James M & Mrs Gertrude M Higgins. Joined the VR in October 1938. Sent to 32 Squadron on 2 July 1940, then to 253 on 9 September.

Victories:	3 Jul	sh/Do17	Destroyed
	20 Jul	Me110	Destroyed
	12 Aug	Me109	Destroyed
	24 Aug	Me109	Destroyed
	11 Sep	Me109	Destroyed
	11 Sep	Me110	Damaged

Sunday, 15 September

Today is recognised as the climax of the Battle of Britain, and is forever known as Battle of Britain Day. Invasion appeared, to the public and the military in Britain, to be imminent, and there had already been several false alarms. Fighter Command had become somewhat stronger in recent days. Dowding, ever mindful of how taxing was the fight, had redeployed his squadrons in order to give each a break from constant alert status, and this allowed the senior pilots a little time to help train newly arrived pilots from OTUs.

It was almost 11 am before the first indications that the Germans were on the move once again with raids starting to come in thick and fast. London was once more the target, met by nine RAF squadrons, including four from the Duxford Wing. Bombs fell in Battersea, Kensington, Lewisham, Crystal Palace, Wandsworth and Westminster. It was the day that a Dornier 17, shot down by 504 Squadron, fell on Victoria Railway Station.

In the afternoon a massive armada of bombers estimated to cover a ten-mile front, headed in off northern Kent. Some 170 RAF fighters met them, from 11 and 10

Groups, and again from the Duxford Wing. London again suffered but the Luftwaffe took terrible losses. German crews had been advised that RAF resistance was soon coming to an end, but they took back estimates of 300 or more fighters meeting them. This was also the day Winston Churchill visited 11 Group's Operations Room at Uxbridge. He could see the massive deployment of Keith Park's fighters and asked what reserves he had. Churchill, at that moment, was told, there weren't any!

Fighter Command lost nearly thirty fighters, but less than a dozen pilots had been killed. The Germans had casualties numbering some 80, of which 56 were lost. That evening the newspaper vendors were shouting that the Germans had lost 185 aircraft, and while this was an exaggeration, their true losses were very significant.

11.50   P/O G L J Doutrepont RAFVR
             229 Sqn
             Hurricane N2537

Shot down over Sevenoaks Kent and crashed on Staplehurst Railway Station. Belgian pilot, aged 27. In 1949 his remains were taken back to Belgium and interred in the Pelouse d'Honneur Cemetery in Brussels. Left Belgium for France in May 1940 but soon decided to get to England, which he did, reaching Liverpool on 7 July. He was commissioned into the VR and joined 229 on 4 August.

Victories:	11 Sep	Do17	Destroyed
	11 Sep	sh/He111	Destroyed

12.10   F/O R Smither RCAF
             1 RCAF Sqn
             Hurricane P3876

Shot down by Me109 over Tunbridge Wells. Canadian from London, Ontario, was 27, and is buried in Brookwood Military Cemetery. His parents were Frank & Mrs Susan Smither, and a brother, Frank, also died in the war on 5 June 1942, flying with 401 Squadron RCAF, shot down by JG26. Ross had joined the RCAF in September 1930.

Victories:	31 Aug	Me109	Damaged
	4 Sep	Me110	Destroyed
	4 Sep	Me110	Damaged

12.20   P/O R A Marchand RAF
73 Sqn
Hurricane P3865

Shot down by Me109 over Maidstone, crashing at Nouds Farm, Teynham. From Beckenham, Kent, he was 22 and is buried in Bromley Hill Cemetery, Lewisham. An original gravestone, placed by his father, was later replaced by CWGC, the original being placed at the crash site on 15 September 1985. He and his wife were injured in a road accident on their honeymoon in May 1940. Joined the RAF in March 1939, posted to 73 in France but wounded on 13 May; married while recovering. Returned to 73 on 6 July.

Victories:	26 Mar	Me109	Damaged
	21 Apr	Me109	Destroyed
	21 Apr	Me109	Destroyed
	13 May	Do17	Probable
	6 Sep	Me109	Destroyed
	11 Sep	Me110	Probable

12.30   P/O G A Langley RAFVR
41 Sqn
Spitfire P9324

Shot down by Me109, crashed at Wick House, Bulphan, near Thurrock. From Stony Stratford, near Milton Keynes, he was 24 and is buried in St Peter & Paul Churchyard, Abington, Northamptonshire. Son of Archibald F M & Mrs Mary E Langley of Northampton. Had joined the VR in March 1939 and went to 41 in Late June 1940. On 11 September he had baled out after his fighter was hit by return fire from a Ju88.

12.30   P/O G N Gaunt AAF (pictured on right)
609 Sqn
Spitfire R6690

Shot down by fighter over south London, crashing near Kenley, Surrey. He was 24 years of age and was buried in Salendine Nook, Baptist Chapel Yard, Huddersfield, Yorkshire. Commissioned into the AAF in April 1940 having been with 609 earlier. Once fully trained he returned to it on 6 August.

Victories:	25 Aug	½ Me110	Destroyed

12.58   P/O J V Gurteen RAFVR
504 Sqn
Hurricane N248

Shot down over south London, crashing near Longfield, south-east of Dartford. From Haverhill, Suffolk, he was 24. His remains were cremated at Hendon Crematorium and his ashes were scattered over his house by F/L W B Royce of 504 Squadron. Son of Conrad S & Mrs Frances A Gurteen of Sturmer, Essex. He had joined the VR in early 1939 and to 504 in late June 1940.

14.45   F/O M Jebb RAFVR
504 Sqn
Hurricane N2705

Shot down over south-east London and crashed near Dartford. Badly injured with burns; died in Dartford hospital on the 19th. Youngest son of Brigadier-General G D Jebb of Hexam, he was 22 and cremated at Hendon Crematorium. Educated at Trinity College, Cambridge, where he served in the University Air Squadron, then commissioned into the VR in September 1938. Arrived on 504 in July 1940.

15.00   Sgt L Pidd RAFVR
238 Sqn
Hurricane P2836

Shot down over Kenley and although he baled out he was dead upon landing. He came from Dunswell, Yorkshire and was 22 years old. Buried in St Peter's Churchyard, Woodmansey, Yorkshire. Son of George R & Mrs Hilda Pidd. Joined the VR in late 1938 and after training was posted to 238 on 18 June 1940.

Victories: 11 Aug   Me109   Destroyed

15.05   F/O A P Pease RAFVR
603 Sqn
Spitfire X4324

Shot down and crashed in Kingswood, near Chartway, Street, Kent. He was 22. Buried in St Michael and All Angels Churchyard, Middleton Tyas, Yorkshire. Son of Sir Richard A Pease JP DL MA 2nd Bart, and Lady Pease of Richmond, Surrey. Educated at Eton and Trinity College, Cambridge, he had been in the University Air Squadron and commissioned into the VR in September 1938. He was posted to 603 on 6 July 1940.

Victories: 30 Jul   sh/He111   Destroyed
           3 Sep   Me109   Destroyed

15.05   Sgt M Brzezowski (pictured on far left)
           303 Sqn
           Hurricane P3577

Lost during combat over the Thames, off Gravesend. From Dawidgrodek, Poland, he was 20, he has no known grave. Awarded the Polish Cross of Valor in December. Made his way to England via Romania and France, flying with Groupe de Chasse II/6 in the latter. Came to England in July 1940; sent to 303 on 21 August.

Victories: 15 Jun   sh/Hs126   Destroyed
           11 Sep   He111   Destroyed
           11 Sep   He111   Destroyed

Non-operational loss

18.20   F/O H M S Lambert RAF
          LAC J P Wyatt RAFVR
          F/O M J Miley RAF
          25 Sqn
          Beaufighter R2067

Flying this Beaufighter with F/O Miley as passenger, crashed near RAF Kenley. The cause has never been established. Lambert was 21, son of a WW1 RFC officer, and was cremated at Henley Road Crematorium, Reading. Joined the RAF in November 1936 after leaving Imperial College. Went to 25 Squadron in August 1937 and as the Battle began he was attached to AFDU and then RAF Biggin Hill for special duties.

Lambert

Wyatt

Miley

Wyatt was 32 years old, son of Arthur & Mrs Beatrice S Wyatt of Rodwell, Weymouth, Dorset. He is buried in Christ Church Churchyard, Melplash, Dorset. He joined the VR in February 1940, going to 25 in late July.

Miley was 22, son of Group Captain Arnold J Miley OBE & Mrs Roberta M M Miley of Felixstowe, Suffolk. His father was air attaché in Buenos Aries. He was buried in St Andrew's Churchyard, North Weald Bassett. He had entered the RAF College at Cranwell in 1936 and went to 25 Squadron in 1938. Attached to AFDU in August 1940.

?   Sgt T R Tweed RAF
          56 Sqn
          Hurricane P3660

During dog-fight practice his aircraft went into a flat spin off the top of a loop. Unable to correct it, Tweed crashed to the ground and was killed. He was flying from Boscombe Down and hit the ground one mile to the north-west of High Post aerodrome, Salisbury. He was 26, son of Thomas & Mrs Lilian M Tweed, and husband to Mrs Nellie Tweed of Worksop, Nottinghamshire.

Monday, 16 September

No operational fatalities

Tuesday, 17 September

It had been quiet on the 16th, with little wonder. However, the 17th saw renewed fighting, but not in the scale of the 15th. Eight RAF fighters were lost but only two pilots killed, a third being lost in an accident. The Germans lost the same number, with a similar number returning home with varying degrees of damage.

15.40   Sgt E J Egan RAFVR
501 Sqn
Hurricane P3820

Shot down by Me109 over Ashford, and crashed in Daniels Wood, near Bethersden. He was from East Dulwich and was 19. Originally noted as 'missing' excavations in later years found that his remains were still at the crash site in 1976 but it was not until 1978 that positive evidence proved to the authorities it was him. An unknown airman's grave was changed to one with his name on it at Brookwood Military Cemetery. Son of James E & Mrs Grace A D Egan of East Dulwich, SE London. Posted to 615 Squadron on 27 August then 501 on 3 September.

Victories: 15 Sep   Me109   Destroyed

15.40   Sgt J Lansdell RAFVR
607 Sqn
Hurricane P3860

Shot down by Hptm. E Neumann of I/JG27 and crashed at The Bell, Beltring, near Tonbridge. He was 23 and is buried in St Margaret's Churchyard, Hempnall, Norfolk. Son of William A & Mrs Ellen S Lansdell of Great Yarmouth. Lansdell had become AFRAeS, with a Diploma in Engineering (1st Class Honours in Aeronautics). He had joined the VR in late 1937 and was posted to 607 in July 1940.

Non-operational loss

16.00   Sgt D A Helcke RAFVR
504 Sqn
Hurricane V7529

Pilot lost control evading dummy attack by RAF fighters above Faversham during practice flight. He baled out but appears to have struck the aircraft and fell dead. This 24-year-old was from Herne Bay, although brought up in South Africa from childhood when his parents moved there. He is buried in

Herne Bay Cemetery, Kent. Son of Walter A & Mrs Marjory Helcke. Came back to the UK in 1935 and studied at Chelsea College, receiving a Diploma in aeronautical engineering. He also became a pilot before joining the VR in early 1939. To 504 Squadron in July 1940.

Victories: 7 Sep   He111   Destroyed

Wednesday, 18 September

German night raids over London and several other major cities heralded another big day of aerial assault. It started with fighter sweeps across Kent, then raids upon Chatham and Rochester by Ju88s followed, escorted by over 100 Me109s. The Duxford Wing was again in evidence but their pilots vastly over-claimed, shooting down about four raiders rather than the thirty they reported shot down. Nevertheless almost twenty Luftwaffe aircraft did not reach their home bases. Twelve RAF fighters were lost but only three pilots died.

09.50   P/O P Howes RAFVR
             603 Sqn
             Spitfire X4323

Shot down by Me109 and fell at Kennington, near Ashford. Aged 21 from Wadebridge, Cornwall, he had attended Oundle and Oxford. He was cremated at St John's Crematorium, Woking, Surrey. Had been with 54 Squadron until moving to 603 on 11 September. Learnt to fly with his University's Air Squadron then joined the VR in June 1939.

12.30   Sgt G W Jefferys RAFVR
             46 Sqn
             Hurricane V7442

Shot down over Clacton, baled out but parachute failed to deploy. From Hemel Hempstead, he was 20 and is buried in St Michael's Churchyard, Winterbourne, Wiltshire. Son of Samuel W & Mrs Henrietta E Jefferys of Winterbourne. Entered the VR in the summer of 1939. He first saw action with 43 Squadron which he joined in July 1940, before moving to 46 on 15 September.

Victories: 2 Sep   Me109   Destroyed
             4 Sep   Me110   Destroyed
             6 Sep   Me109   Destroyed
             15 Sep   sh/Do17   Destroyed

13.25 F/L D G Parnall RAF
249 Sqn
Hurricane V6685

Shot down over Gravesend crashing near Furness Farm, Furze Hill, Margretting, Essex. Aged 25, he is buried in St Genesius' Churchyard, St Gennys, Cornwall. Son of George G & Mrs Edith R Parnall of St St Gennys. Parnall had achieved a BA (Cantab) with Downing College, Cambridge. RAFVR in January 1938, receiving a commission into the RAF in September. Posted to 249 on 28 May 1940.

Victories:	8 Jul	sh/Ju88	Destroyed
	15 Aug	Me110	Destroyed
	2 Sep	Me110	Destroyed
	7 Sep	sh/He111	Destroyed
	11 Sep	sh/He111	Destroyed

Thursday, 19 September

No operational fatalities

Friday, 20 September

Just small fighter sweeps on this day which cost the RAF seven fighters and four pilots. German losses were just one Me109 shot down and another seriously damaged in a crash landing at Cap Gris Nez.

10.20 P/O D F Holland RAFVR
72 Sqn
Spitfire X4410

Shot down over Canterbury, crashing at Stiff Street, near Sittingbourne. Baled out severely wounded and died soon after being admitted to hospital. He was 23 and from Berkshire. Buried in St Andrew's Churchyard, Chaddlesworth, Berkshire. Civil Air Guard pre-war, and was the youngest flying instructor in Britain, instructing at the Portsmouth Aero Club. When joining the VR in 1938 he had some 3,000 flying hours in his log book.

Victories:	15 Aug	Ju88	Probable
	4 Sep	Me110	Destroyed
	5 Sep	Me109	Destroyed
	5 Sep	Me109	Damaged
	15 Sep	He111	Destroyed

11.15   P/O H L Whitbread RAF
              222 Sqn
              Spitfire N3203

Shot down by Me109 and crashed at Pond Cottage, Hermitage Farm, Higham, Rochester. Born Ludlow, he was 26 and buried in Ludlow New Cemetery, Shropshire. Son of Herbert H & Mrs Alice Whitbread of Ludlow. Commissioned into the RAF in March 1939, he joined 222 on 6 November 1939.

Victories: 9 Sep   Me109   Destroyed

11.34   P/O H P Hill RAF
              92 Sqn
              Spitfire X4417

Shot down by Maj. W Mölders of JG51 over Dungeness, crashing at West Hougham. The Spitfire landed in high tree tops, not being found until a month later. From Christchurch, New Zealand, he was 20 years old and is buried in Folkestone Cemetery. Son of Jack S & Mrs Dorothy H Hill of Spring Creek, Marlborough, NZ. Went to Marlborough College 1932-36, applied for the RAF in 1938 and sailed for England in December. Once trained he joined 92 in October 1939.

Victories:	26 Jul	½ Ju88	Destroyed
	15 Sep	He111	Destroyed
	15 Sep	He111	Destroyed
	15 Sep	½ Do17	Destroyed
	18 Sep	Ju88	Destroyed
	19 Sep	½ Ju88	Probable
	19 Sep	½ Ju88	Damaged

11.34   Sgt P R Eyles RAF
              92 Sqn
              Spitfire N3248

Shot down by Maj. W Mölders of JG51 off Dungeness. From Basingstoke, he was 24, but has no known grave. Son of Ralph S & Mrs Grace E Eyles of Basingstoke, Hampshire. Entered the RAF as an apprentice in 1932 until 1935. Later applied for pilot training and eventually got a posting to 92 Squadron on 23 October 1939.

Victories:	2 Jun	He111	Damaged
	11 Sep	He111	Destroyed

Non-operational loss

11.30   Sgt C V Meeson RAFVR
              56 Sqn
              Hurricane L1595

Crashed near Bulford Camp, near Amesbury, Wiltshire, as a result of a flying accident during formation practice. He was buried in Loughton Cemetery, Essex. CWGC has him listed as being with 249 Squadron. From Loughton he joined the VR in June 1939 and was posted to 56 on 31 August.

Saturday, 21 September

No operational fatalities

Sunday, 22 September

No operational fatalities

Monday, 23 September

More fighter sweeps by Me109s in the early morning and late afternoon cost the RAF eight fighters and two pilots, but the 109s suffered nine losses.

11.30   Sgt D H Ayers RAFVR
              74 Sqn
              Spitfire P7362

Baled out during routine patrol south-east of Southwold, cause unknown. Lost at sea but his body was recovered on 4 October, and he is buried in Ipswich Cemetery, Suffolk. From Herne Bay, Kent he was 26, the son of Frank K & Mrs Edith M Ayres. Joined 74 on 23 September having been with 600 Squadron earlier.

?   P/O W Beaumont DFC RAFVR
              152 Sqn
              Spitfire R7016

Failed to return, believed to have crashed into the Channel. He came from Dewsbury, Yorkshire, was 26, and has no known grave. Son of Fred & Mrs Delia Beaumont, and husband to Doris J N Beaumont of Coulsdon, Surrey. He had achieved a BSc at the University of London, and joined the University Air

Squadron in January 1937. Thought to have been the first member of the RAFVR, with service number 740000. Joined 152 early in 1940. On 27 August he baled out into the sea after being hit by return fire from a Ju88. His DFC was gazetted on 22 October.

Victories:	12 Aug	sh/Me109	Destroyed
	12 Aug	Ju88	Damaged
	12 Aug	Ju88	Damaged
	16 Aug	Me109	Destroyed
	16 Aug	Me109	Destroyed
	18 Aug	Ju87	Destroyed
	18 Aug	Ju87	Destroyed
	18 Aug	½ Me109	Destroyed
	22 Aug	Ju88	Destroyed
	25 Aug	Me109	Destroyed
	27 Aug	½ He111	Destroyed

Tuesday, 24 September

Today saw the start of the Luftwaffe's change of tactics to attack aircraft factories, the one at Southampton (Woolston factory) being attacked. It was seriously damaged and one bomb hit a shelter, killing 98 employees and injuring some 40 others. Only one of the attacking Me110s was shot down, and that to AA fire.

09.00   P/O J S Bryson RAF
         92 Sqn
         Spitfire X4037

Shot down by Me109 near North Weald. A Canadian from Westmount, Montreal, he was 27. Buried in St Andrew's Churchyard, North Weald Basset, Essex. Son of John T & Mrs Marion E Bryson of Montreal, Canada. Had previously been in the Royal Canadian Mounted Police, joining the RAF in January 1939. To 92 Squadron on 20 October.

Victories:	2 Jun	He111	Damaged
	24 Jul	sh/Ju88	Destroyed

16.30   P/O W J Glowacki
         605 Sqn
         Hurricane P3832

Shot down over French coast by Me109, and captured but wounded. He later died of blood poisoning and was buried in Guines Communal Cemetery. He was 26. Had been with 145

Squadron in mid-August, moving to 605 on the 31st. Escaped to England from Poland in late 1939.

Victories: 11 Sep   Me110   Destroyed
                11 Sep   sh/He111   Destroyed

Wednesday, 25 September

More strong attacks this day, one of which was against the Filton aircraft works at Bristol. Thinking the attack would head for the Yeovil works of the Westland Aircraft Company, RAF fighters were sent towards it, leaving Filton devoid of fighter cover. Again a factory had been hard hit with 250 casualties among the workers, and 107 elsewhere.

11.50   Sgt W G Silver RAF
               152 Sqn
               Spitfire P9463

Missing in action over Portsmouth, his home town. He was 27 and was buried in Milton Road, Cemetery, Portsmouth. Joined the RAF in 1929 as an aircraft apprentice (fitter). Selected for pilot training he was initially a ferry pilot until posted to 152 in July 1940.

12.00   Sgt K C Holland RAFVR
               152 Sqn
               Spitfire N3173

Crashed near Church Farm, Bristol during attack on He111s west of Bristol. An Australian from Sydney, he was 20 years old and living in Camelford, Cornwall. He was cremated at Weymouth Crematorium. Son of Harold G & Mrs Gladys C Holland, and ward of Mr H I E Ripley of Camelford. Joined the VR in 1939 having studied at the Airspeed Aeronautical College 1936-37. Posted to 152 Squadron in June 1940.

Victories: 17 Sep   sh/Ju88   Destroyed
                19 Sep   Ju88   Destroyed
                25 Sep   He111   Damaged

21.30   P/O E Orgias RAF (top left)
Sgt L R Karasek RAF (top right)
AC2 R I Payne RAFVR (bottom)
23 Sqn
Blenheim L8369

Stalled and crashed coming in to land and crashed at Broughton near Stourbridge, Wiltshire. All three men killed. Orgias, who was 25, son of Albert E & Mrs Edith H Orgias of Napier, Hawke's Bay, New Zealand, had reported he was returning from a night patrol with a rough engine. He held a diploma in sheep farming from Massey Agricultural College, Palmerston North NZ. Buried in St Peter's Churchyard, Over Wallop.

Karasek, aged 23, is also buried in Over Wallop. He joined the RAF in mid-1939 and arrived on 23 Squadron on 30 July 1940.

Payne was 31, the son of William & Mrs Edith Payne of Treeton, near Sheffield. He was buried in St Helen's Churchyard, Treeton. He had been a coal miner, so in a reserve occupation, but still volunteered for the RAF when war started and was called up in June 1940. Joined 23 Squadron on 23 September, killed two days later.

Thursday, 26 September

Today was the turn of the factory at Woolston again; this time He111s with escorting Me110s made up the attack force in the late afternoon. Thirty-seven people died, three Spitfires were destroyed in the works, and a further twenty or so damaged. Three RAF pilots were lost.

11.00   P/O W M C Samolinski
253 Sqn
Hurricane V7470

Failed to return from combat action over the Channel. Polish pilot, he was 23 and has no known grave. Arrived from Poland in late 1939 and commissioned into the RAF in January 1940. Joined 253 on 16 July.

Victories:	30 Aug	Me110	Destroyed
	4 Sep	Me110	Destroyed

16.30   Sgt V Horsky
              238 Sqn
              Hurricane P3098

Shot down by Me110 over the Solent. Czechoslovakian pilot, he was 26 years old and has no known grave. Born in Bruchotin and joined the Czech Air Force. Escaped to France and then England. Joined 238 on 12 September.

16.50   Sgt J McB Christie RAFVR
              152 Sqn
              Spitfire K9882

Shot down by Me109 off Swanage. Body picked up and buried in Arkleston Cemetery, Renfrew, Scotland. Son of Alex & Mrs Margaret Christie of Oldhall, Paisley, Scotland. Joined the VR in July 1938 and eventually 152 in August 1940.

Friday, 27 September

Today saw another heavy assault against Britain, raiders being reported on their way in by 08.15 hours. Enemy aircraft came in across the coast from Dover to Brighton, but remained over Kent and Surrey in an attempt to have RAF fighters exhaust fuel and ammunition in order that another planned attack on London would have an easier time. However, a mix-up at the rendezvous point left the raiding bombers at the mercy of RAF fighters – 55 bombers against 120 British fighters. Calls for help from the bomber crews brought in 109s and 110s and Fighter Command suffered losses, but a dozen bombers had been brought down. Twenty-eight fighters were lost and twenty pilots were killed.

09.15   F/O O J Peterson RCAF
              1 RCAF Sqn
              Hurricane P3647

Shot down in combat over Hever, Kent. An American from Eckville, Atlanta, he was 25 years old and buried in Brookwood Military Cemetery. Son of Peter & Mrs Magdalene Peterson, and husband of Helen M Peterson of Halifax, Nova Scotia, Canada. Studying at the University of Saskatchewan he achieved a BA Degree. Joined the RCAF in November 1938.

Victories:	1 Sep	Do17	Damaged
	4 Sep	Me110	Damaged
	9 Sep	Me109	Destroyed
	25 Sep	sh/Do17	Destroyed

09.20   F/L J A Paterson RAF
               92 Sqn
               Spitfire X4422

Shot down over Sevenoaks, falling at Sparepenny Lane, Farningham. A New Zealander from Dunedin, he was 20, and had seen action over France. Buried in Star Lane Cemetery, Orpington, Kent. For his services during the French campaign, he was made MBE in the 1941 New Year's Honours List being engaged on reconnaissance missions in a Magister. Son of Samuel B & Mrs Fannie Paterson of East Chatton, Southland, NZ. Pre-war he was a trooper with the Otago Mounted Rifles, then joining the RNZAF; began flying with the Otago Flying Club in 1938. He had baled out of his burning Spitfire on 11 September, suffering burns to his face but insisted on returning to duty.

Victories:	24 Jul	sh/Ju88	Destroyed
	19 Aug	sh/Ju88	Destroyed
	11 Sep	Me110	Destroyed

09.25   F/L L H Schwind RAF
               213 Sqn
               Hurricane N2401

Shot down in combat over Gatwick, crashing onto Wildernesse Golf Course, Seal, near Sevenoaks. He was 27 and is buried in Crowborough Burial Ground, Sussex. Son of Charles L & Mrs Florence Schwind of Crowborough, Sussex and husband to Mrs Georgina Schwind. With the RAF in the late 1930s he had served in the Middle East. Joined 257 Squadron on 1 September, then 43 Squadron on the 10th and finally 213 on the 20th.

09.35   F/O L W Paszkiewicz DFC
               303 Sqn
               Hurricane L1696

Shot down and crashed at Crowhurst Farm, Borough Green, Kent. He was 22 and flew in Poland and France. Buried in Northwood Cemetery. Awarded the DFC in 1941, and the Polish Virtuti Militari and Cross of Valour. Polish Air Force pre-war and then fought in France, joining 303 in England on 2 August 1940. His first victory was achieved during a training flight, breaking formation to make the interception. It was 303's first kill and he was both admonished and congratulated.

Victories:	30 Aug	sh/Me110	Destroyed
	7 Sep	Do17	Destroyed
	7 Sep	Do17	Destroyed
	11 Sep	Me110	Destroyed
	15 Sep	Me109	Destroyed
	26 Sep	He111	Destroyed

09.35   Sgt T Andruszkow
303 Sqn
Hurricane V6665

Shot down over the Horsham area, and crashed at Holywych Farm, Cowden. From Lwow, Poland. He was 19, and is buried in Northwood Cemetery. Fought in Poland before going to France and then England. After shooting down a Dornier on 15 September he was himself shot down by a Me109 and baled out.

Victories:	15 Sep	sh/Do17	Destroyed
	26 Sep	He111	Destroyed

09.40   P/O E E Males RAFVR
72 Sqn
Spitfire X4340

Shot down by Me109 over London, crashing at Shadwell Dock, Stepney. From Southgate, London, he was 20 years old and is buried in Great Northern London Cemetery (Southgate). Son of Charles A & Mrs Rose Males of Southgate, Middlesex. Had joined 72 on 19 June 1940. On 4 September he was forced to bale out after his fighter was set on fire in a fight with Me110s, and also had to make a forced landing on the 25th, hit by return fire from the Dornier.

Victories:	2 Sep	Me109	Destroyed
	10 Sep	sh/Do215	Destroyed
	14 Sep	Me109	Destroyed

09.40   F/Sgt C Sydney RAF
92 Sqn
Spitfire R6767

Shot down and crashed at Kingston-on-Thames, Surrey. Came from St Mary Cray, aged 25 when he died. Buried St Mary Cray Cemetery, Orpington, Kent. Son of Mr & Mrs H Sydney of St Mary Cray, Orpington, husband to Mrs Ellen J M Sydney. Aircraft apprentice from September 1930 (metal rigger) then pilot training from 1933. Served with 19 and 266 Squadron prior to 92.

Victories: 15 Sep   Me109   Destroyed

09.40   F/O P J Davies-Cooke RAF
72 Sqn
Spitfire N3068

Shot down over Sevenoaks, Kent, crashing at West Wickham. He baled out but fell dead. Aged 23, from Flintshire (Clwyd) he is buried in St John's Churchyard, Rhydmwyn, Cilcain, Flintshire. Son of Mr & Mrs P T Davies-Cooke of Mold, Flintshire. After Cambridge, he joined the Auxiliary Air Force in 1937, then the RAF as a university entrant in 1939. After being with 613 Squadron he volunteered to fly fighters, went to 610 Squadron then 72 on 20 September.

09.50   F/O P R-F Burton RAFVR (pictured on right)
249 Sqn
Hurricane V6683

Collided with a Me110 over Redhill area and crashed at Hailsham. He was a South African from Cape Province, aged 23, and is buried in St Andrew's Churchyard, Tangmere. Served in the South African Coast Garrison and Citizen Forces in 1935. Came to UK and to Christ Church Cambridge, where he was reserve cox in the 1938 University Boat Race. Learned to fly with the University Air Squadron and joined 249 on 21 July 1940.

It was thought that Burton had deliberately rammed the 110 after using all his ammunition and although there was talk of a Victoria Cross, all he received was a mention in despatches. His father was a former Union Minister for Finance and Railways.

Victories: 2 Sep   Do17   Probable
6 Sep   Ju88   Damaged
26 Sep   Do17   Damaged
27 Sep   Me110   Destroyed

10.30   Sgt L A Dyke RAFVR
             64 Sqn
             Spitfire X4032

Failed to return. From Sutton, Surrey, he was 22 and has no known grave. His parents were Arthur St.C & Mrs Ada M Dyke of Sutton, Surrey. Joined the RAFVR in mid-1939, and joined 64 in September 1940.

11.45   P/O R F G Miller RAF
             609 Sqn
             Spitfire X4107

Collided head-on with a Me110 of Chesilbourne, near Kingscombe, Bournemouth. From Radford Semile, Warwickshire, he was 20. His remains were buried in St Nicholas' Churchyard, in his home town. He had joined the RAF in June 1939 and was posted to 609 on 4 May 1940.

Victories:	13 Jul	Do17	Damaged
	12 Aug	Me110	Damaged
	13 Aug	Ju87	Destroyed
	24 Sep	sh/Do17	Destroyed
	25 Sep	sh/He111	Destroyed
	27 Sep	Me110	Destroyed

12.20   F/O D S Smith RAF
             616 Sqn
             Spitfire R6702

Shot down by Me109, crashing near Faversham badly wounded. Taken to the local cottage hospital but died the next day. He came from Highley, Shropshire, was 26 years old and is buried in St Mary's Churchyard in Highley. Son of Major Frederick C & Mrs Florence L Smith. His victory on 27 June 1940 was achieved at night, one of the few by a Spitfire pilot in darkness. Joined the RAF in April 1938 while a school teacher. After training he was attached to the Fleet Air Arm, but posted to 616 in early 1940, seeing action over Dunkirk.

Victories:	1 Jun	Ju88	Damaged
	27 Jun	He111	Destroyed
	15 Aug	sh/Ju88	Destroyed
	30 Aug	Me109	Destroyed

12.25   F/O M G Homer DFC RAF
242 Sqn
Hurricane P2967

Shot down in combat and crashed near Sittingbourne, Kent. He had won his DFC with 44 Squadron in April 1940 for bombing operations. He came from Swanage, Dorset, aged 21, and is buried in his home town cemetery. Son of George J W & Mrs Millicent Homer. Volunteering for fighters he flew with 1 Squadron prior to a move to 242 on 21 September. A Cranwell cadet from January 1937 his first unit had been 106 Squadron.

Victories: 7 Sep   Do17   Damaged

12.25   P/O E M Gunter RAFVR
501 Sqn
Hurricane V6645

Show down over Sittingbourne, Kent. Baled out but parachute failed to deploy. From Holmsley, Hampshire, aged 20. Son of William H and Mrs Margery Gunter. Buried at St Mary's Churchyard, Aldeby, Norfolk, where his father was Vicar. Joining the VR in May 1939, he had been briefly with 257 and 43 Squadrons before joining 501 on 22 September 1940.

12.30   P/O E Burgoyne RAF
19 Sqn
Spitfire X4352

Shot down by Me109 over Canterbury, crashing at Coldred, Kent. He was 25 and buried in St Mary's Churchyard, Burghfield, Berkshire. Son of Leonard & Mrs Nina Burgoyne of Burghfield Common. Joined the RAF just before the war and posted to 19 Squadron in June 1940.

Victories: 31 Aug   sh/Me110   Destroyed

12.45   P/O P M Cardell RAFVR
603 Sqn
Spitfire N3244

Possibly wounded in action over the Channel, attempted to get home but had to bale out just off Folkestone. Parachute failed to open and his body was recovered by a fellow pilot who had seen him go into the sea, force-landed on the beach and commandeered a boat. From Huntingdonshire, he was 23 and was buried in Holy Trinity Churchyard, Great Paxton. He had joined the VR in May 1939 and posted to 263 Squadron on 23 June 1940. A few days later he moved to 603. The pilot who tried to rescue him was Flying Officer P G Dexter DFC who was killed over France in July 1941.

Victories: 27 Sep   Me109   Destroyed

15.18   Sgt T G Oldfield AAF
              92 Sqn
              Spitfire R6622

Shot down over Dartford, Kent. Buried in St Stephen's Church Burial Ground, Chertsey, Surrey. He was 21. Served as an aircraft hand in 615 Squadron pre-war and, becoming a pilot after war began, went to 64 Squadron in early September 1940, then to 92 soon afterwards.

15.20   P/O J R B Meaker DFC RAF (pictured on left)
              249 Sqn
              Hurricane P3834

Shot down by return fire from a Ju88, crashed at Brake Field, Gifford's Farm, Dallington. He baled out but hit the tailplane and fell dead. He came from Kinsale, Co. Cork, aged 21, buried West Dean Cemetery, Sussex. His parents were Edgar R & Mrs Lucy A K Meaker of West Dean, Sussex. Joined the RAF in June 1939, joining 46 Squadron at the end of March 1940, and went to Norway with it in May. Back in the UK he was moved to 249 Squadron in June. DFC gazetted 8 October 1940.

Victories: 15 Aug   Me110   Destroyed
               24 Aug   Me109   Destroyed
               2 Sep   Do17   Damaged
               2 Sep   ½ Do17   Destroyed
               2 Sep   Me110   Destroyed
               6 Sep   Me109   Destroyed
               6 Sep   Me109   Destroyed
               15 Sep   Do17   Destroyed
               15 Sep   Do17   Destroyed
               15 Sep   ½ Do17   Probable
               15 Sep   Me109   Damaged
               27 Sep   ½ Me110   Destroyed

15.30   F/L R F Rimmer RAF
              229 Sqn
              Hurricane V6782

Shot down and exploded over Franchise Manor Farm, Burwash. From Meols, Cheshire he was 21. He is buried at the Grange Cemetery, Hoylake, Cheshire. Son of Lancelot & Mrs Cecilia Rimmer of Meols. His father had been in the RFC in WW1 and later flew with Sir Alan Cobham's Flying Circus. Pre-war he gave pleasure flights along the Welsh coast and during WW2 was a test pilot at Speke, as the family lived at Wirral, Cheshire before moving to Meols. No doubt influenced by his father's flying career, Rimmer joined the RAF in March 1937 and joined 66 Squadron in November 1937. After Dunkirk he moved to 229.

Victories:	2 Jun	He111	Damaged
	15 Sep	Do17	Destroyed
	15 Sep	sh/He111	Destroyed

16.00   Sgt E Scott RAF
              222 Sqn
              Spitfire P9364

Missing. For many years permission to excavate the crash site at Hollingbourne was refused but finally in 1990, following representation by Prince Charles, it was, and Scott's remains were recovered and buried with full military honours at Margate Cemetery, Kent. He had come from Mansfield, Nottinghamshire, and was aged 22 when he died. He was shot down by Maj. W Mölders of JG51. Son of Mrs E M Scott & stepson of Mr L Kent of Mansfield, Nottinghamshire. Joined the RAF in 1935. Posted to 222 Squadron in March 1940.

Victories:	3 Sep	Do17	Destroyed
	3 Sep	Me109	Destroyed
	5 Sep	Me110	Probable
	5 Sep	Me109	Destroyed
	7 Sep	Me109	Destroyed
	9 Sep	Me109	Probable
	11 Sep	He111	Destroyed
	27 Sep	Me109	Destroyed

Saturday, 28 September

Today would see losses of sixteen RAF fighters and ten pilots, for claims of two Me109s. The Germans lost some bombers but not to fighter attack. The Germans were employing smaller numbers of bombers but ensuring they were escorted by larger numbers of Me109s.

10.10   P/O F C Harrold RAF
                  501 Sqn
                  Hurricane P3417

Crashed at College House, Ulscombe, Kent, following combat with 109s. Came from Cambridge and is buried at Cherry Hinton (St Andrew) Churchyard near his home. He was 23 years old. Son of Frederick C & Mrs Florence N Harrold. He had been with 25 and 151 Squadrons earlier, moving to 501on 26 September.

10.20   F/L H K MacDonald AAF
                  603 Sqn
                  Spitfire L1076

Shot down over Gillingham, Kent by Me109, falling on to Brompton Barracks. Cremated at Warriston Crematorium, Edinburgh, aged 28. His parents were James H & Mrs Isa M K Macdonald of Murreyfield, Edinburgh. He had become a BA (Cantab) at college. His victory on 26 June was achieved at night. He had joined the AAF in 1935, flew with 603, and then with it when called to full time service as war started.

Victories:	16 Oct '39	sh/Ju88	Destroyed
	19 Jan	sh/He111	Destroyed
	7 Mar	sh/He111	Destroyed
	25/26 Jun	He111	Destroyed
	31 Aug	Me109	Destroyed
	6 Sep	Me109	Probable
	7 Sep	He111	Destroyed
	18 Sep	Me109	Destroyed
	23 Sep	Me109	Probable
	27 Sep	Me109	Destroyed

10.30   P/O H H Chalder RAFVR
41 Sqn
Spitfire X4409

Baled out over Charing seriously wounded, landing at Garling Green, Kent. Died in Chartham Hospital near Canterbury, 10 November. Aged 25, he is buried in St Nicholas' Cemetery, Newcastle-upon-Tyne. Joined the RAF in 1935, going to 266 Squadron in April 1940. Moved to 41 Squadron on 15 September.

10.37   F/O J G Boyle RAF
41 Sqn
Spitfire X4426

Shot down over Chilham, Kent, crashing on Erriots Farm, Dadmans, Lynsted. A Canadian from Castelmain, Ontario, he is buried in Lynsted New Churchyard at St Peter & St Paul. He was the 26-year-old son of Dr Joseph P Boyle BA & Mrs Catherine G Boyle of Ottawa, Canada. As the war began he was with 611 Squadron. Moving to 41 the following year. He had joined the RAF in August 1937 and then been with No.1 Air Observer's School at North Coates.

Victories:	11 Aug	sh/Ju88	Destroyed
	5 Sep	Me109	Destroyed
	9 Sep	He111	Destroyed
	15 Sep	Me109	Destroyed
	15 Sep	¼ Do17	Destroyed
	17 Sep	Me109	Destroyed
	17 Sep	Me109	Destroyed

13.55   F/O P G Crofts RAF
605 Sqn
Hurricane V6699

Shot down by Me109 over Ticehurst, Sussex. Baled out but fell dead near Dallington, probably a victim of strafing in the air. A Londoner, he was 22 and a Cranwell Cadet. He is buried in All Saints Churchyard, Tilford, Surrey. Son of Lt-Colonel Leonard & Mrs Margaret Crofts of Waverley, Surrey. Entered RAF Cranwell in January 1937; did not complete the course but took a short service commission in 1938.

Although trained for bombers he volunteered for Fighter Command and was sent to 615 Squadron, moving to 605 on 13 September.

14.45   Sgt R Little RAFVR
               238 Sqn
               Hurricane N2400

Shot down into the sea by Me110 off the Isle of Wight. He was 23 and from Cumberland, but has no known grave. He was the son of Robert & Mrs Marian R Little of Armathwaite, Cumberland, where they ran the Red Lion Hotel. Joined the VR in August 1939, and 238 Squadron in May 1940. On 13 August he was shot down by a 109, baled out over the sea and was rescued unharmed.

Victories:	11 Jul	sh/Me110	Probable
	8 Aug	Do17	Damaged
	15 Sep	sh/Ju88	Destroyed
	15 Sep	He111	Damaged
	25 Sep	He111	Destroyed

14.50   P/O D S Harrison RAFVR
               238 Sqn
               Hurricane P3836

Shot down by Me109 over the Solent and crashed into the sea. His body was washed ashore at Brighton on 9 October, and buried in St Andrew's Churchyard, Tangmere. He came from Sidcup, Kent and was 29 years of age. His parents were Gerald S & Mrs Lizzie M Harrison of St Leonards-on-Sea, Sussex, and he was married to Mrs Ruth Harrison. RAFVR in January 1939 and joined 238 on 12 September.

14.59   Sgt S E Bann RAFVR
               238 Sqn
               Hurricane V6776

Baled out during combat with Me109s over Brading Marshes, but his parachute failed to deploy. From Macclesfield, he was 26, and was buried in his local cemetery. Son of Samuel & Mrs Credence Bann, and husband to Mrs Agnes M Bann of Birmingham. Joined the VR in May 1938, joining 238 Squadron in June 1940.

Victories:	13 Jul	Me110	Destroyed
	11 Aug	He111	Destroyed
	13 Aug	He111	Destroyed
	21 Sep	sh/Ju88	Destroyed

15.00   F/L W E Gore DFC AAF
607 Sqn
Hurricane P3108

Shot down by Me109 off Selsey Bill. From Stockton-on-Tees, he had flown Gladiators in the French Campaign. He was 25 but has no known grave. Son of George E & Mrs Edith Gore of Brighton, Sussex. He achieved a BSc at Durham University and became an electrical engineer before joining 607 Auxiliary Squadron in 1934. Served in France with this unit and his DFC was gazetted on 31 May. Wounded in France.

Victories:	10 May	sh/He111	Probable
	11 May	sh/He111	Destroyed
	12 May	sh/He111	Destroyed
	12 May	sh/He111	Destroyed

15.00   F/L M M Irving AAF (pictured third from right)
607 Sqn
Hurricane R4189

Crashed into the sea off Selsey following combat with Me109s. From Jesmond, Northumberland, he was 29 and has no known grave. Son of Benjamin & Mrs Kathleen Irving, and husband of Mrs Sheila Irving of Jesmond. Joined the Auxiliary Air Force (607 Sqn) in 1933, having already obtained a private pilot licence. Went to France in November 1939.

Victories:	14 Sep	sh/Ju88	Destroyed

Sunday, 29 September

18.30   F/O G C B Peters RAF
                   79 Sqn
                   Hurricane P5177

Failed to return from interception of He111 over the Irish Sea. His body was later recovered and was buried in Rathnew Cemetery, Co. Wicklow. He was 27 years old. Son of George H B & Mrs Marion Peters of Aldwick, Sussex. Joined the RAF in December 1938 and 79 Squadron in August 1940.

Victories:	15 Aug	Me110	Destroyed
	30 Aug	He111	Destroyed
	4 Sep	sh/Me110	Destroyed
	7 Sep	Do17	Damaged

Non-operational loss

?   P/O J McGibbon RAFVR
        615 Sqn
        Hurricane V7312

During a routine practice flight, his fighter suddenly dived into the ground from 7,000 feet, cause not known, but perhaps oxygen failure. He was 24, the son of James McGibbon CMG & Mrs McGibbon of Shandon, Scotland. He had joined the VR in March 1939 and eventually found himself with 615 Squadron at Prestwick on 23 September. He was killed six days later.

Monday, 30 September

A large early morning raid, numbering around 200 aircraft, crossed the Kent coast west of Dover soon after 9 am, heading for London. Twelve RAF squadrons intercepted them and many of the raiders were turned away by the time they had reached Maidstone, costing them three bombers and four 109s. Three Hurricanes were shot down. Later fighter sweeps were flown across Weymouth Bay but strong RAF fighter forces prevented any of them getting too far inland.

Another attempt on London came after lunch and some reached the city, but escorting 109s of JG27 suffered losses of eight fighters and five pilots. Other German fighter units lost two dozen 109s, while bomber losses amounted to a dozen. Some of these occurred during an attack on the Westland factory at Yeovil in the late afternoon. Many bomber crews were unable to identify their target and jettisoned their bomb loads.

10.30   Sgt A F Laws DFM RAF
          64 Sqn
          Spitfire P9564

Killed in a collision while on patrol north of Leconfield. He came from East Derham, Norfolk, and was 28. Buried in Wells-next-the-Sea, Norfolk as a pilot officer. His DFM was gazetted on 1 October 1940 that had been recommended on 26 August and announced on 17 September. He had joined the RAF in 1931 as an aircraft hand and served in the Middle East. He volunteered for pilot training while in Egypt and joined 64 Squadron in April 1936. He continued to serve with 64 when it returned to the UK.

Victories:	12 Jun	½ He111	Destroyed
	29 Jul	Me109	Destroyed
	11 Aug	Me109	Damaged
	13 Aug	Do17	Damaged
	15 Aug	Me109	Destroyed
	18 Aug	½ He111	Destroyed
	18 Aug	Me110	Destroyed

10.40   F/O M Ravenhill RAF (pictured in the middle)
          229 Sqn
          Hurricane P2815

Shot down by Me109, falling at Church Road, Ightham, near Sevenoaks. He was 27 and is buried in City Road, Cemetery, Sheffield, his home town. Joined the RAF in March 1938 and trained in Egypt. Posted to 229 Squadron on 9 March 1940. He had been shot down on 1 September and suffered from shock after baling out.

13.30   P/O J D Crossman RAF
              46 Sqn
              Hurricane V6748

Shot down by German fighter, falling at Tablehurst Farm, Forest Row, Sussex. An Australian from Mossman, Queensland, he was 21 years of age. Buried in Chalfont St Giles Churchyard, Buckinghamshire. Son of George E & Mrs Gladys A Crossman of New Lambton, New South Wales. On his second attempt he was accepted for a short service commission in the RAF in mid-1939, sailing for the UK in August. Posted to 46 Squadron on 12 September.

Victories: 15 Sep   Do17   Probable

16.45   Sgt L A E Reddington RAFVR
              152 Sqn
              Spitfire L1072

Missing during combat off Portland. He was 26 and came from Coundon, Warwickshire. He was married to Georgina M Reddington of Allesley, Warwickshire, with whom he already had a daughter. A second daughter arrived in February 1941, named Lesley after her father. He has no known grave. His parents were Arthur and Mrs Lillian M Reddington. Joined the VR in 1938, going to 152 Squadron in July 1940.

17.00   F/O J R Hardacre RAF
              504 Sqn
              Hurricane P3414

Shot down over the south-west coast of Hampshire. Body washed ashore on the Isle of Wight on 10 October and buried in All Saints Churchyard, Fawley, Hampshire. He came from Birmingham, and was 24, son of James W & Mrs Marion E Hardacre of Ruislip, Middlesex. He had flown in France, and had been shot down twice on 16 May, crash-landing once and then baling out. His log-book recorded five German aircraft destroyed and two damaged.

Victories:

15 May	Ju87	Destroyed
15 May	Ju88	Destroyed
19 May	Me109	Damaged
7 Sep	Me110	Destroyed
15 Sep	Do17	Destroyed

21.40 Sgt C Goodwin RAFVR (left)
Sgt G E Shepperd RAF (right)
AC2 J P McCaul RAFVR
219 Sqn
Blenheim L1261

Flying a night patrol their aircraft disintegrated due to unknown causes. Goodwin from Hull was 21, son of Mr & Mrs C Goodwiin, and was buried in Hull Northern Cemetery. Shepperd, from Sidcup, Kent, was 23, the son of George & Mrs Fanny E Shepperd, and stepson to Annie E Shepperd. He was buried in the RAF Catterick Cemetery. McCaul was 28 and was buried at Leigh Cemetery, Lancashire.

Non-operational loss

? F/O C H Bacon RAFVR
610
Spitfire

Killed in a flying accident, his fighter crashing on Alnmouth Beach, Northumberland. He was 21, son of William C & Mrs Charlotte Bacon of Windermere. He was a Demy at Magdalen College, Oxford, which is a form of scholarship unique to that college. He was buried at St Mary's Cemetery, in Windermere, Cumbria.

Chapter 10

October 1940

Tuesday, 1 October

10.50   F/L C E Bowen RAF
              607 Sqn
              Hurricane P2900

Shot down in combat with Me110s over the Isle of Wight. From Chelsea, London, this 24-year-old has no known grave. Son of Charles B & Mrs Linda R E Bowen of Chelsea, London. Joined the RAF in a short service commission in December 1936. After a period of instructing and then with 615 Squadron, he moved to 607 while they were in France in 1940. On 26 September he was shot down over the Isle of Wight, baled out and landed safely. He had been made a flight commander on 3 September.

Victories:	15 Aug	2/He111s	Destroyed
	15 Sep	Do215	Destroyed
	15 Sep	sh/Do17	Destroyed
	30 Sep	Me110	Damaged

10.50   Sgt N Brumby RAFVR
              607 Sqn
              Hurricane V6686

Shot down over the Isle of Wight in fight with Me110s. From Kingston-upon-Hull, he was 22 at the time of his death. Buried in Hull Northern Cemetery, Yorkshire. Joined the RAF in 1938 and was with 103 Bomber Squadron but volunteered for fighters in 1940. With 615 and then 607 Squadrons, on 31 September.

11.10   Sgt F A Sibley RAFVR
              238 Sqn
              Hurricane P3599

Missing over Poole Harbour after fight with enemy fighters. He was 26 years old and has no known grave. Son of Bernard & Mrs Kate M Sibley of Hull. Joined the VR in summer of 1939, going to 238 on 19 August 1940.

?	P/O C C Bennett RAF (left) Sgt G B Brash RAF (right) Sgt G S Clarke RAFVR 248 Sqn Blenheim R3626

Missing from reconnaissance off Norwegian Coast. No known graves. Bennett was from Mallala, South Australia. He was aged 23, the son of Septimus B & Mrs Catherine M Bennett of Mile End, Adelaide, South Australia. Brash was from Edinburgh, the son of David & Mrs Margaret Brash. Clarke, from Bedford, was 19 and son of Harold Henry and Mrs Doris Clarke.

Victories (Bennett): 28 Sep   Do18   Damaged
(The Dornier in fact landed on the sea, and sank after the crew abandoned it.)

Wednesday, 2 October

No Operational fatalities

Thursday, 3 October

03.55	P/O C A Hobson RAF (left) Sgt D E Hughes RNZAF (right) AC2 C F Cooper RAFVR 600 Sqn Blenheim L4905

Suffered engine failure during patrol in heavy rain and hit trees at Broadstone Warren, Forest Row, Sussex. Hobson was 21, son of George C & Mrs May V Hobson of Monxton, Hampshire. Buried All Saints Churchyard, Banstead, Surrey.

Hughes was from Dunedin, New Zealand, and was 28, the son of David A & Mrs Jimima, of Kaponga, Tanranaki, NZ. Buried in St Luke's Churchyard, Whyteleafe, Surrey. Cooper was from Heath Town, Wolverhampton, son of Enoch & Mrs Amelia Cooper and was buried in Holy Trinity Churchyard, Heath Town. He was 20 years of age.

Friday, 4 October

16.00   F/L K McL Gillies RAF
66 Sqn
Spitfire X4320

Failed to return from an interception of a He111 off east coast. Body washed ashore at Covehithe, Suffolk, on 21 October. From Liverpool, he was 27 and is buried in the Thornton Garden of Rest, Lancashire. His parents were R W & Mrs Mary R Gillies of Great Crosby, Liverpool. Joined the RAF in 1939, going to 66 in December 1936. The next year he was part of the Squadron's team at the Hendon Air Display. Following a period with 254 Squadron he returned to 66 in April 1940 seeing action in France and over Dunkirk.

Victories:	13 May	Ju87	Destroyed
	13 May	Me109	Damaged
	2 Jun	Ju88	Damaged
	20 Aug	sh/Me110	Destroyed
	31 Aug	sh/Do17	Destroyed
	15 Sep	½ He111	Probable
	15 Sep	He111	Damaged
	15 Sep	sh/Do17	Destroyed
	18 Sep	s½ He111	Destroyed
	18 Sep	Me109	Damaged
	23 Sep	Me109	Damaged
	27 Sep	Me110	Probable
	27 Sep	sh/Do17	Destroyed
	27 Sep	sh/Do17	Destroyed
	27 Sep	sh/Do17	Destroyed
	30 Sep	Me109	Probable
	30 Sep	Me109	Destroyed

Saturday, 5 October

09.50   P/O N Sutton RAFVR
72 Sqn
Spitfire K9989

Mid-air collision soon after take-off from Biggin Hill and died in the crash. Born in Bradford, but lived in St Helens, he was 26, and is buried in his local cemetery. Son of Oliver & Mrs Florence Sutton, husband of Joan Sutton of St Helens, Merseyside. Played Rugby Union for his home town and joined the AAF pre-war. Initially with 611 Squadron he moved to 72 on 29 September 1940.

12.00   F/O W Januszewicz
              303 Sqn
              Hurricane P3892

Shot down by Me109, falling at Stowting, Kent. This Polish pilot was 27 and had fought in Poland. Buried in Northwood cemetery, Middlesex.

Sunday, 6 October

12.07   Sgt A Siudak
              303 Sqn
              Hurricane P3120

Killed during bombing attack by lone raider as he was taxiing at RAF Northolt. Aged 31, he is buried at Northwood Cemetery, Middlesex.

14.20   Sgt F F Vinyard RAFVR
              64 Sqn
              Spitfire R6683

Crashed into the sea during patrol, cause not known. He has no known grave. From Erdington, Birmingham, he was 24. Son of Frederick H & Mrs Annie L Vinyard. Joined the VR in the spring of 1940 and had just joined 64 when he was killed. Served previously with the Polish Air Force and later with the French. Posted to 302 Squadron on 23 July 1940, moving to 303 on 23 September. Awarded a posthumous Virtuti Militari on 1 February 1941. He was aged 31 and is buried in Northwood Cemetery.

Victories:	15 Sep	sh/Do17	Destroyed
	5 Oct	Me110	Destroyed
	5 Oct	Me109	Destroyed
	5 Oct	Me109	Destroyed

Monday 7 October

10.40   F/O N J M Barry RAFVR
              501 Sqn
              Hurricane V6800

Shot down by Me109 over Wrotham, Kent. From Franschhoek, South Africa, aged 22. Baled out but fell dead and is buried in St Andrew's Churchyard, Finhall, Yorkshire. He was the son of

Richard A & Mrs Gladys I Barry of Keer Weder, Franschhoek, Cape Province. Had been to Pembroke College, Cambridge, flew with the University Air Squadron and transferred to the RAFVR. After serving as ADC to AVM Champion de Crespigny, he asked for a posting to a fighter squadron, going to No.3 in July 1940. He joined 501 Sqn on 26 September.

10.45　　F/O H K F Matthews RAF
　　　　　　603 Sqn
　　　　　　Spitfire N3109

Shot down by Fw. W Roth of 4/JG26 and crashed at Godmersham, Kent. He was 28 and cremated at Beckenham Crematorium, his remains are interred in Crystal Palace District Cemetery. Joined the RAF in November 1937 serving with 64 Squadron from September 1938. In June 1940 he moved to 54 Squadron then posted to 603 on 30 September, but only lasted a week.

Victories:	9 Jul	sh/He59	Destroyed
	12 Aug	Me109	Destroyed
	25 Aug	Me109	Destroyed

14.00　　P/O C E English RAF
　　　　　　605 Sqn
　　　　　　Hurricane V7305

Shot down by Me109 south of London, crashing at Brasted. From Newcastle-on-Tyne, he was 28 and is buried in St Andrew's and Jesmond Cemetery, Newcastle-on-Tyne. His fighter pilot brother was killed in action in North Africa in May 1941. They were sons of Joseph & Mrs Bertha E English.

16.00　　F/O I B Difford RAF
　　　　　　607 Sqn
　　　　　　Hurricane L1728

Killed following mid-air collision during a patrol, crashing at Slindon, Sussex. From Johannesburg, South Africa, he was 30, and buried in St Andrew's Churchyard, Tangmere. Son of Captain Ivor D & Mrs Elfrida G Difford. Joined the RAF in 1937 and saw service in the Far East, not arriving in England until September 1940. First going to 85 Squadron he quickly moved to 607 on 2 October and was killed five days later.

16.30   Sgt A N Feary RAFVR
609 Sqn
Spitfire N3238

Shot down by Me109 over Yeovil. Baled out too low and was killed. From Derby, he was 28 and is buried in Holy Trinity Churchyard, Warmwell. Son of Thomas & Mrs Maud V of Derby. Joining the VR in October 1938 his first Squadron was No.600, but moved to 609 on 11 June 1940.

Victories:	18 Jul	sh/Ju88	Destroyed
	12 Aug	Me109	Destroyed
	13 Aug	Ju87	Destroyed
	13 Aug	Me110	Damaged
	14 Aug	Ju88	Destroyed
	25 Aug	Me110	Destroyed
	25 Aug	Me110	Damaged
	7 Sep	Me109	Probable
	7 Sep	Ju88	Damaged
	24 Sep	Do17	Destroyed
	25 Sep	Do17	Damaged

16.40   P/O H J Akroyd RAF
152 Sqn
Spitfire N3039

Shot down during attack on bombers over Lyme Regis, crashed at Nutmead, Shillingstone, Dorset. Akroyd was badly burned and died on the 8th. Buried Holy Trinity Churchyard, Warmwell. He was 27 years old. He had joined the RAF in January 1937 and had gone to 152 at the start of the Battle.

Victories:	15 Aug	Ju87	Destroyed

16.50   P/O J W Broadhurst RAF
222 Sqn
Spitfire P9469

Shot down during attack on bombers and crashed at Bailey's Reed Farm, Hurst Green, Salehurst. Baled out but fell dead at Longhurst, Sussex. Son of Sam & Mrs Charlotte A Broadhurst, and husband to Edith L Broadhurst of Bexley, Kent. He came from Crayford and was 23 years of age. Posted to 222 in October 1939, converting to Spitfires in March 1940.

Victories:	31 Aug	Me109	Destroyed
	4 Sep	Me109	Destroyed
	7 Sep	Me109	Destroyed
	27 Sep	Me109	Destroyed

17.50   Sgt B E P Whall DFM RAFVR
              602 Sqn
              Spitfire X4160

After being hit by return fire from a Ju88 off Beachy Head, he spun in attempting a forced landing near Lullington, Sussex. Taken to Eastbourne Hospital badly injured he died while being admitted. He was 22 and is buried in St Mary's Churchyard, Amersham, Bucks. His parents were Mr & Mrs Nevill A Whall of Paddington, London. Joined the VR in mid-1937, and just after war started went to 605 Squadron. In April he moved to 263 Squadron, sailing to Norway to operate Gladiators on a frozen lake. He was also part of a second expedition there in May and for these two efforts he received the DFM (24 September 1940). Sent to 602 Squadron he saw action, being forced to ditch when his aircraft was hit by return fire from a bomber on 18 August.

Victories:	23 May	Do17	Destroyed
	?	EA	Destroyed
	?	EA	Destroyed
	16 Aug	¼ Do17	Destroyed
	18 Aug	Ju87	Destroyed
	18 Aug	Ju87	Destroyed
	26 Aug	He111	Destroyed
	26 Aug	He111	Destroyed
	7 Sep	Me109	Destroyed
	9 Sep	Do17	Destroyed
	30 Sep	¼ Ju88	Destroyed
	30 Sep	Ju88	Probable
	7 Oct	½ Do17	Probable

Tuesday, 8 October

09.30   P/O G H Corbett RAFVR
              66 Sqn
              Spitfire R6779

Shot down by Maj A Galland of JG26 south of Eastchurch. Canadian from Saskatchewan and later British Columbia, he was 21, and is buried in St Mary's Churchyard, Upchurch, Kent. He was the son of Henry C & Mrs Mabel Corbett of Oak Bay, Victoria, BC. His family had emigrated to Canada in 1914, and returned in the late 1930s. Corbett enrolled into the De Havilland Aircraft Construction School, and learning to fly joined the VR in late 1937. Joined 66 on 26 July 1940.

Victories:	27 Sep	Ju88	Destroyed

09.40 Sgt J Frantisek DFM VM KW
303 Sqn
Hurricane R4175

Crashed at Ewell, Surrey during patrol. Born in Dolni in Lower Otaslavice, Czechoslovakia, he was one day past his 27th birthday. He is buried in Northwood Cemetery. Fought in Poland and France. Posthumously commissioned a 1st Lieutenant in 1945.

Victories:	2 Sep	Me109	Destroyed
	3 Sep	Me109	Destroyed
	5 Sep	Me109	Destroyed
	5 Sep	Ju88	Destroyed
	6 Sep	Me109	Destroyed
	9 Sep	Me109	Destroyed
	9 Sep	He111	Destroyed
	11 Sep	He111	Destroyed
	11 Sep	Me109	Destroyed
	11 Sep	Me109	Destroyed
	15 Sep	Me110	Destroyed
	18 Sep	Me109	Destroyed
	26 Sep	He111	Destroyed
	26 Sep	He111	Destroyed
	27 Sep	Me110	Destroyed
	27 Sep	He111	Destroyed
	30 Sep	Me109	Destroyed
	30 Sep	Me109	Probable

11.55 Sgt R A Ward RAFVR
66 Sqn
Spitfire N3043

Shot down by Me109 over North Kent, falling near Rochester. From Croydon, he was 23 and buried in Mitcham Road Cemetery, Croydon. Joined the AAF in 1936, transferring to the VR a year later. Initially with 19 Squadron in August 1940 he moved to 616 on 5 September and then to 66 on the 29th.

12.05 Sgt J R Farrow RAFVR
229 Sqn
Hurricane V6820

Lost control in cloud during a patrol over Bovington. Machine fell to pieces at 200 feet. From Eastleigh, aged 24, son of John R & Mrs Constance M Farrow of Eastleigh, Hampshire, he is buried in Northwood Cemetery. His education brought him a BSc degree.

21.20   P/O H I Goodall RAFVR
Sgt R M B Young RNZAF
264 Sqn
Defiant N1627

Crashed at Marlow, Bucks, having called to report he was investigating a suspected enemy aircraft. Goodall was 25 and is buried at Parkstone Cemetery Poole, Dorset. His parents were John & Mrs Harriet G Goodall. Young was from Palmerston North, New Zealand, son of John C & Mrs Emma H Young. He was 22 and was buried in Northwood Cemetery, Middlesex.

Victories:	25 Aug	Ju88	Destroyed
	26 Aug	Do17	Destroyed

Non-operational loss

15.40   P/O D Hastings RAF
74 Sqn
Spitfire P7329

Collided with Spitfire P7373 during practice attacks over base at RAF Coltishall. Came down inverted south of Green Farm, Gillingham, Norfolk. The son of Francis & Mrs Mary A Hastings of North Shields, Tynemouth, he was buried in Preston Cemetery, Tynemouth. He had joined the RAF in June 1939, and the following year was assigned to go to a Hurricane squadron in France, but instead was posted to No. 74 Squadron. He was 25.

Victories:	11 Aug	Me109	Destroyed
	11 Aug	Me109	Damaged
	13 Aug	Do17	Destroyed
	13 Aug	Do17	Probable
	11 Sep	Me110	Probable

15.40   P/O F W Buckland RAF
74 Sqn
Spitfire P7373

Collided with Spitfire P7329 making dummy attacks over Coltishall and crashed at Ivy House Farm, Gillingham, Norfolk. He was the 20-year-old son of Herbert H & Mrs Bessie M Buckland of Brighton, Sussex. He was cremated at the Woodvale Crematorium, Brighton.

Wednesday, 9 October

12.50   Sgt E T G Frith RAFVR
92 Sqn
Spitfire X4597

Baled out over Ashford after combat being badly burned. Died in hospital on the 17th and buried in Oxford Cemetery, Botley, Berkshire. He came from Cowley and was 26, the son of Arthur R & Mrs Sarah Frith. Joined the VR in 1938, and posted to 92 Squadron on 21 September 1940.

17.30   P/O J C Kirkpatrick RAFVR (pictured right)
P/O R C Thomas RAFVR
Sgt G E Keel RAFVR (pictured below right)
235 Sqn
Blenheim N3530

Missing after combat action over the Channel. Probably shot down by Uffz. H-J Frölich of JG26, who survived a crash-landing at Sangatte, where his 109 burned out. Kirkpatrick was Belgian, aged 25. He arrived in England in June 1940, joining 235 on 5 August. Thomas came from Cardiff, and his body was recovered and buried in Cathays Cemetery, Cardiff. Keel's body too was recovered and buried in Highland Road Cemetery, Eastney, Portsmouth. He was 20 and the son of Allen G & Mrs Gertrude A Keel of Southsea. He had joined the VR in mid-1939, joining 235 on 13 August 1940.

Non-operational loss

11.15   Sgt S Warren RAFVR
1 Sqn
Hurricane V7376

Failed to return from a section cloud formation exercise over the Wash and came down in the sea. This 22-year-old was the son of Mrs Ethel Warren, of Hull, and has no known grave. He had joined the VR in August 1939 and had only been posted to 1 Squadron on 21 September.

Thursday, 10 October

08.15   P/O D G Williams RAF
        92 Sqn
        Spitfire X4038

Killed in mid-air collision while attacking a Do17 over Tangmere. He was 20 years old and is buried in London Road Cemetery, Salisbury, Wilts. Joined the RAF in February 1939, posted to 92 Squadron on 23 October. Saw action over Dunkirk, shooting down his first enemy aircraft on his first operational sortie.

Victories:		
23 May	Me110	Destroyed
23 May	Me110	Probable
23 May	Me110	Probable
2 Jun	He111	Destroyed
10 Jul	He111	Probable
26 Jul	½ Ju88	Destroyed
14 Aug	He111	Destroyed
14 Aug	½ He111	Probable
11 Sep	He111	Destroyed
15 Sep	Do17	Damaged
15 Sep	Do17	Damaged
15 Sep	Do17	Destroyed
15 Sep	He111	Destroyed
29 Sep	Do17	Damaged
30 Sep	Do17	Probable
4 Oct	Ju88	Damaged

08.15   F/O J F Drummond RAF
        92 Sqn
        Spitfire R6616

Collided with P/O D G Williams during attack on Do17 over Tangmere. Baled out injured but too low for his parachute to deploy. He came from Liverpool, was 21, and is buried in Thornton Garden of Rest, Lancashire. His parents were William H & Mrs Nellie Drummond of Blundellsands, Liverpool. He joined the RAF in April 1938. Posted to 46 Squadron on 14 January 1939, he and several other pilots were presented to HM King George V for their actions over a North Sea convoy on 21 October, during which three He115s were shot down and another forced to land on the water. He went with 46 to Norway in May 1940 and was awarded the DFC (26 July). On 5 September he moved to 92 Squadron.

Victories:		
29 May	He111	Destroyed
2 Jun	Ju87	Destroyed
7 Jun	He111	Destroyed
7 Jun	He111	Destroyed

7 Jun	He111	Damaged
7 Jun	He111	Damaged
11 Sep	Me109	Probable
23 Sep	Me109	Destroyed
24 Sep	Me109	Probable
24 Sep	Me109	Damaged
24 Sep	Ju88	Damaged
27 Sep	sh/Me110	Destroyed
27 Sep	Ju88	Destroyed
30 Sep	Me109	Probable
5 Oct	Me109	Destroyed
5 Oct	Hs126	Destroyed

12.20   Sgt J Hlavac
56 Sqn
Hurricane P3421

Shot down by Me109 over Wareham. From Petrvald, Czechoslovakia, he was 26 and is buried in Holy Trinity Churchyard, Warmwell. He had escaped to Poland and then to France, and finally to England in June 1940. Posted to 79 Squadron on 11 September, then to 56 on 8 October.

15.47   Sgt E A Bayley RAFVR
249 Sqn
Hurricane V7537

Crashed near Cooling Marsh, Kent. From Rye, he was 29 years of age and was buried in St Luke's Cemetery, Bromley, Kent. Son of Edward G & Mrs Edith Bayley, and husband of Josephine A Bayley of Hailsham, Sussex. In Canada in 1929-30 he studied agriculture and back in the UK he joined the VR in December 1937. On 1 June 1939 he was sent to 32 Squadron moving to 249 on 17 September. The cause of the crash is not known but it was possibly due to enemy action. Excavating the crash site in 1982 some bullet marks were found so he may well have been shot down by Fw. Reins of I/JG2 who claimed a Hurricane at this time and location.

Victories:	3 Jul	sh/Do17	Destroyed
	18 Aug	Do215	Destroyed

15.55   Sgt H H Allgood RAF
253 Sqn
Hurricane L1928

Crashed into houses at Albion Place, Maidstone, Kent. Cause not known. He came from Cambridge, and is buried at St Mark's Burial Ground in his home town. He

was 25. His brother, F/Sgt E A Allgood RAFVR was lost over the North Sea flying with 120 Squadron, Coastal Command, on 28 May 1942. Their parents were James & Mrs Florence All good. Allgood joined the RAF as an apprentice metal rigger in August 1934, volunteering for pilot training in September 1938. Posted to 85 Squadron in France on 14 May 1940, he was later posted to 253 in 28 September.

Victories: 11 Aug Me109 Destroyed

?   Sgt O Hanzlicek
312 Sqn
Hurricane L1547

Baled out when his fighter caught fire during a patrol over the river Mersey. He landed in the river and drowned. He was aged 29, born in Ústí nad Labem. He is buried in West Derby Cemetery, Liverpool. Escaping from Czechoslovakia he joined the French Air Force and flew with Groupe de Chasse II/5, with Curtiss Hawk 75s. From them he received the French Croix de Guerre, and the Czech Military Cross from his own people. Came to England via North Africa and Gibraltar, ending up with 312 on 19 September. The Hurricane L1547 was a well-worn machine dating back to 1937, that went through production trials and then to 111 Squadron, a unit testing Hurricane aircraft thoroughly.

Victories: 23 Apr Do17 Probable
                11 May He111 Destroyed
                18 May sh/Me109 Destroyed

Friday, 11 October

16.00   Sgt C A H Ayling RAF
421 Flt
Spitfire P7303

Shot down in combat, falling near Hawkinge. He was 28 and is buried in St Nicholas' Cemetery, Moncton, Pembroke. He had been an aircraft apprentice in September 1927 and later trained as a pilot. As the war began he was with 43 Squadron and on 7 June 1940 he crash landed in France but managed to get himself back to England flying a Hurricane with punctured fuel tanks. He went to 66 Squadron on 10 September, then 421 Flight on 8 October. His brother, LAC A E Ayling RAFVR died on 19 August 1942. They were sons of Mrs Amelia Ayling of Cowplain, Hampshire.

Victories: 12 Jul sh/He111 Destroyed

16.24   F/O D H O'Neill RAF
              41 Sqn
              Spitfire X4042

Climbing to engage Me109s he collided with another Spitfire. Baled out but his parachute failed. He was 25 and is buried in Streatham Park Cemetery, Mitcham, Surrey. Son of Lt-Colonel Edward M & Mrs Ethel M O'Neill of Glasnevin, Co Dublin, and husband to Muriel O'Neill. Joined the RAF in July 1938, to 611 Squadron on 20 August 1940, then to 41 on 29 September.

16.30   P/O J G Lecky RAF (pictured far left, on wing tip)
              41 Sqn
              Spitfire P9447

Shot down by Me109 over Maidstone. Baled out but killed. He was born in Japan, his father working at the British Embassy. He was 19 and is buried in All Saints Churchyard, Tilford, Surrey. Son of Lt-Colonel John G & Mrs Marion D H G Lecky of Lower Bourne. Entered the RAF College at Cranwell in April 1939 as a flight cadet and was commissioned in March 1940. After a brief stay in an army co-op squadron he was posted to 610 Squadron in August, moving to 41 on 1 October.

19.45   Sgt K C Pattison RAFVR
              611 Sqn
              Spitfire P7323

Shot down by return fire from Do17s, near Kidderminster. He was badly injured and died in hospital on the 13th. Buried Nottingham Southern Cemetery, West Bridgeford. He was 27. Joined the RAF in November 1938 and posted to 611 on 23 September.

Victories: 11 Oct   Do17   Destroyed

Saturday, 12 October

09.20   P/O H R Case RAFVR
              72 Sqn
              Spitfire P9338

Crashed at Capel-le-Ferne, near Folkestone while on patrol, cause not known. From Withycombe, Somerset, aged 24, he is buried in St Nicholas Churchyard in his home town. Joined the Squadron on 20 September. He was the son of Edgar F & Mrs Mary A Case. Joined the VR in June 1936. After training he joined 64 Squadron on 28 August, moving to 72 on 20 September.

10.40   Sgt J V Wadham RAFVR
            145 Sqn
            Hurricane V7426

Shot down by Me109 over Hastings, Sussex, falling near Cranbrook. He came from the Isle of Wight, and is buried in Carisbrooke Cemetery, in Newport. He was 21, son of Victor S & Mrs Lilian O Wadham of Newport, IoW. Joined the VR in November 1938. Served with 601 Squadron from 3 August, then moved to 145 on the 20th.

12.30   Sgt P R C McIntosh RAFVR
            605 Sqn
            Hurricane P3022

Shot down by Me109 off Dungeness. 20-year-old son of John G and Mrs Florence McIntosh of Croydon, Surrey. Buried in Shirley (St John) Churchyard, Surrey. Born Brockley, Avon, he joined the VR in February 1939. Posted to 151 Squadron in July 1940 then moved to 605 on 3 September.

16.40   F/O A J S Pattinson RAF
            92 Sqn
            Spitfire X4591

Shot down by Me109 over Hawkinge. Born in Chelsea, London, he lived in Bournemouth and is buried in Parkestone Cemetery, Poole, Dorset. He was 21, son of John F & Mrs Daphne StG S Pattinson of Fordingbridge, Hampshire. Joined the RAF in December 1937 and 23 Squadron in July 1940. Sent to 92 on 5 September.

21.40   Sgt G M Head (safe)
            P/O R V Baron RAFVR
            219 Sqn
            Blenheim L1113

Engine trouble during night patrol and crew baled out. Head landed safely, but Baron, who was 40 years of age and came from Highbury, London, died as his parachute failed. Aircraft crashed at Ewhurst, Sussex. Baron is buried in Sittingbourne and Milton Cemetery. Son of Mr & Mrs Ernest E L Baron, and husband to Pansy Louise Baron. Baron had volunteered for aircrew duties in April 1940 and joined 219 in June. Geoffrey Head was killed, still with 219 Squadron on 8 February 1941.

Sunday, 13 October

18.00   Sgt R E Stevens RAFVR
AC2 A Jackson RAFVR
Sgt O K Sly RAFVR
29 Sqn
Blenheim L6637

Shot down by 312 Czech Squadron in error, crashed into the sea off Point of Aire, near the Morecombe Light. Stevens was 20 and came from Croydon. Joined the VR in February 1939, going to 29 in June 1940. Jackson was 29 and the radar operator. He was the son of Arthur & Mrs Rose H Jackson of Mexborough, Yorkshire. He had gone into the VR in June 1940, and been sent to 29 in August. Sly was from Weston-super-Mare, aged 20, son of Frederick W & Mrs Blanche C Sly. Having joined the VR in August 1939 he had been posted to 29 exactly a year later. They have no known graves.

Monday, 14 October

12.50   F/O R Hope RAF
605 Sqn
Hurricane P3107

In poor weather conditions he chased a German bomber into the Inner Artillery Zone and collided with a balloon cable, crashing at South Norwood. He was a second cousin to Neville Chamberlain, born in Birmingham, aged 26. Went to Eton and Oxford, becoming a rowing blue in 1935. Cremated at St John's Crematorium, Woking. Son of Donald & Mrs Beth Hope, husband of Diana B Hope of Chelsea, London.

Victories: 9 May   ½ Do17   Destroyed

Tuesday, 15 October

08.15   Sgt S A Fenemore RAFVR
501 Sqn
Hurricane V6722

Shot down by Me109 over Redhill, Surrey, crashing near Godstone. From Whitewell, Co. Antrim, NI, was 20 years old, son of W A and Mrs Gertrude Fenemore. Entered the VR in February 1939, and went to 245 Squadron in July 1940. Moved to 501 in September. Buried in Allerton Cemetery, Liverpool.

09.00   Sgt P D Lloyd RAFVR
              41 Sqn
              Spitfire X4178

Shot down by Hauptmann J Foezoe of 4/JG51, falling into the Channel. He came from Loughton, Essex, aged 23. His body was washed ashore in Herne Bay on the 27th and was buried in Holy Innocents Churchyard, High Beach, Essex. Son of James & Mrs Elizabeth K Lloyd of Loughton and husband to Phyllis I Lloyd. Joined the VR in September 1938 and 41 Squadron one year later.

10.00   Sgt K B Parker RAFVR
              92 Sqn
              Spitfire R6838

Shot down by Me109 over the Thames Estuary falling into the sea. From Worthing, Sussex, he joined the RAFVR in 1938. After brief service with 64 Squadron he moved to 92 on 24 September. Son of Herbert G and Mrs Winifred M Parker, husband to Stella M D Parker. His body was washed ashore and buried in Terschelling General Cemetery, The Netherlands.

Victories: 24 Sep   Me109   Probable

11.45   F/L I J Muirhead DFC RAF
              605 Sqn
              Hurricane N2546

Shot down by Me109 over Maidstone, crashing near Gillingham. Born in West Ham, London, in 1913, his family later moved to Carlisle. He became an aircraft apprentice in 1929, passed out in 1932 and later applied for pilot training. NCO with 151 Squadron pre-war then sent to 605 Squadron in April 1940. Saw action prior to the Battle and received the DFC, the first by a 605 pilot. He was 27 when he died and is buried in St Mary's Churchyard, Holme Cultram, Cumberland. Son of John S and Mrs Clara Muirhead, of Abbey Town.

Victories:		
10 Apr	He111	Damaged
22 May	He111	Damaged
22 May	He111	Destroyed
25 May	Hs126	Destroyed
25 May	Ju87	Destroyed
25 May	Ju87	Destroyed
26 May	Me110	Destroyed
15 Aug	½ He111	Destroyed
24 Sep	½ Do17	Destroyed
7 Oct	Me109	Damaged

13.05 P/O P S Gunning RAF
46 Sqn
Hurricane N2480

Shot down by Me109 over Thames Estuary, crashing at Little Thurrock. He was 29 and is buried in St Andrew's Churchyard, North Weald Bassett. He joined the RAF in 1932, commissioned in April 1940 and posted to 46 in early July.

13.30 F/Sgt E E Williams RAF
46 Sqn
Hurricane V6550

Shot down by Me109, and crashed in Gravesend. From Taplow, Bucks, was an RAF aircraft apprentice in 1928. Passed out in 1931 and requested pilot training in 1934. Began pilot training in 1939, and his first unit was 29 Squadron. Moved to 46 in 1940. Son of William and Mrs Amelia Williams, husband to Joan Margaret Williams. He was 28 and has no known grave.

Wednesday, 16 October

No Operational fatalities

Non-operational loss

? Sgt S J Chalupa RAF
310 Sqn
Hurricane P3143

Crashed near Ely, Cambridgeshire, while engaged on a routine training flight, cause not known. From Brno, Czechoslovakia, he was 21 years old.

Thursday, 17 October

09.00 P/O N N Campbell RAF
242 Sqn
Hurricane V6575

Presumed shot down by Do17 off Yarmouth and went into the sea. From Ontario, his first unit was 32 Squadron in May 1940 then moved to 242 at Biggin Hill before going to France. Aged 27, he has no known grave. Son of Alexander J & Mrs Isabella G

Campbell of St Thomas, Ontario, Canada. Joined the RAF in January 1939, joining 32 Squadron in late May 1940. Moved to 242 on 3 June, and operated over France until 18 June. His body was recovered and is buried in Scottow Cemetery, Norfolk. He was aged 27 when he died.

Victories:	18 Sep	Ju88	Destroyed
	18 Sep	sh/Ju88	Destroyed
	18 Sep	sh/Ju88	Destroyed

10.05   Sgt J Zaluski
302 Sqn
Hurricane V7417

Overturned while attempting a forced landing at Collier's End, Hertfordshire. Escaping from Poland, this 23-year-old joined the RAF in February 1940. Posted to 302 on 21 September. Buried in Northwood Cemetery. His Hurricane was repaired and was used for training at 55 Operational Training Unit until the end of the war.

15.25   P/O H W Reilley RAF
66 Sqn
Spitfire R6800

Shot down by Maj W Mölders of JG51 over Westerham, Surrey. Born London, Ontario, this Canadian came to England and joined the RAF in May 1939. Buried in Gravesend Cemetery, Kent, aged 22. His parents were Hugh W & the late Mrs Annie Reilley of Detroit, Michigan, USA. His first Squadron had been No. 64 in early September moving to 66 on 15 September.

Victories:	27 Sep	Me109	Destroyed

15.40   F/O A L Ricalton RAF
74 Sqn
Spitfire P7360

Shot down by Me109 over Maidstone, Kent. From Gosforth, Newcastle-upon-Tyne, he was 26. During the Battle of France he flew battles with No. 142 Squadron with the AASF. Volunteered to fly fighters in August, going to 74 on 21 August. Received a mention in despatches. Buried in Sittingbourne Cemetery. Son of William & Mrs Margaret J Ricalton of Gosforth.

16.30   P/O R Atkinson RAFVR
213 Sqn
Hurricane P3174

Shot down by Me109, crashing near Puckley, near Egerton, Kent. Born Gillingham, Kent his first posting was to 242 Squadron going to France with this unit until June. Following brief spells with both 600 and 111 Squadrons, he went to 213 on 19 September. Aged 25, he is buried in Northwood Cemetery. He was the son of Gilbert & Mrs Florence E Atkinson.

Victories: 30 Sep   Me109   Destroyed

Friday, 18 October

Pm   Sgt E E Shepperd RAF
152 Sqn
Spitfire R6607

Crashed at Tadnoll Hill, near Dorchester, cause not known. From Binstead Isle of Wight, he was 23. With 152 from October 1939. Buried in his home town cemetery in Ryde. Son of the late Joseph E (died in 1919 as a result of wounds received in WW1) and Mrs Ada K Shepperd of Ryde. Joined the RAF as an apprentice in September 1933, passing out as a wireless mechanic in 1936. Later he applied for pilot training.

Victories:

25 Jul	Me109	Destroyed
12 Aug	Ju88	Destroyed
18 Aug	Ju87	Destroyed
30 Sep	Ju88	Destroyed
7 Oct	Ju88	Destroyed

16.05   P/O S Wapniarek
302 Sqn
Hurricane P3872

Crashed while attempting forced landing in bad weather near Thames Ditton, returning from a patrol. This 24-year-old Pole fought during the Polish campaign and received the Virtuti Militari, and Cross of Valour. Buried Northwood Cemetery. Polish Air Force cadet, he flew with 132 Squadron during the Polish campaign, before escaping to England.

Victories:

1 Sep '39	Me109	Destroyed
15 Sep '39	Do17	Destroyed
16 Sep '39	Hs126	Destroyed
18 Sep '40	Ju88	Destroyed

16.05   P/O A Zukowski
             302 Sqn
             Hurricane V6571

Crashed near Detling, running out of fuel in bad weather while returning from a patrol. After the Polish campaign, escaped to France and fought with Groupe de Chasse I/45. He was 29 years old and is buried in Northwood Cemetery. Awarded the Cross of Valour in December.

Victories:	10 Jun	Do17	Destroyed
	10 Jun	Do17	Destroyed

16.10   F/O P E G Carter RAF
             302 Sqn
             Hurricane P3931

Crashed at Kempton Park Race Course returning from patrol in bad and foggy weather. Baled out too low and was killed. Had served with 605 and 73 Squadrons, the latter in France; then attached to 302 on 24 August. Buried in Queen's Road Cemetery, Croydon. Son of Harry G and Mrs Eugene W Carter of West Croydon. He was 21.

Victories:	10 Apr	sh/He111	Destroyed
	24 May	Me110	Destroyed
	15 Aug	Ju88	Destroyed
	15 Aug	Ju88	Destroyed

16.10   F/O J Borowski
             302 Sqn
             Hurricane P3930

Crashed on Kempton Race Course returning from patrol in bad weather. Joined 302 on 17 October and this was his first operation. He was 28 and is buried at Northwood Cemetery. Joined 302 on 17 October, so died just one day later.

Saturday, 19 October

?   Sgt L C Allton RAFVR
             92 Sqn
             Spitfire R6922

Crashed near Smarden, Kent, circumstances not recorded although his name appears in the 'killed in action' records. From Nuneaton he was 20 years of age, and had seen action in France on bombers. After a brief spell with 266 Squadron he moved to 92 on 30 September. Buried in the Oaston Road Cemetery in his home town. He was the son of Charles & Mrs Beatrice A Allton. Joined the VR in March 1939 and joined 98 Squadron in May 1940. Converted to Spitfires and posted to 226 on 3 September, and 92 on the 30th.

Sunday, 20 October

am P/O S R Gane RAF (pictured)
P/O M D Green RAFVR
Sgt N J Stocks RAF
248 Sqn
Blenheim L9453

Missing from recce mission to Norwegian Coast. Gane came from Dunoon, Argyllshire, aged 20, the son of Lieutenant Sidney R A P C & Mrs Dora D S Gane of Dunoon, Argyllshire. His body was recovered and was buried in Stavne Cemetery, Trondheim, Norway. Joined the RAF in March 1939, and 248 in February 1940. Green, also 20, had joined the VR in August 1939 and 248 on 30 March 1940. Stocks joined as a boy entrant in May 1938, re-mustering as a Wop/AG and joined 248 in late July 1940. Green and Stocks have no known graves.

09.30 F/L G M Baird RAF (pictured)
Sgt R Copcutt RAF
Sgt D L Burton RNZAF
W/O S V Wood RAF
248 Sqn
Blenheim P6952

Shot down in combat off Norwegian Coast. They had engaged a Do215 which they shot down, but then three Me109s attacked them and forced them to ditch. F/L G M Baird (NZ), W/Off D L Burton and W/Off S V Wood were taken prisoner. Copcutt (Observer) was lost and has no known grave. He came from Whetstone, Middlesex and was 20 years old. His parents were Thomas E & Mrs Ada E Copcutt. This crew had been searching for L9453.

14.55   Sgt T B Kirk AAF
              74 Sqn
              Spitfire P7370

Shot down in combat with fighters over Maidstone. Baled out severely wounded and eventually succumbed to his injuries in July 1941. Aged 22 he is buried in East Harlsey Churchyard, Yorkshire, his home town. He was the son of Thomas H and Mrs Esther Kirk. Joined 608 AAF Squadron as an aircraft hand in June 1939, and re-mustered as an airman under training. Then joined 74 on 26 August 1940.

Victories: 11 sep   Me110   Destroyed

Monday, 21 October

12.50   P/O W S Williams RAF
              266 Sqn
              Spitfire X4265

Took off to intercept raiders near Cambridge but upon returning, he had to land for fuel at Stradishall. Later he took off and as he flew low over the airfield he seemed to stall, his engine cut out, and he crashed. From Dunedin, New Zealand, he had joined the RAF in June 1938 and sailed for England in February 1939. Joined 266 in November. He was 20 years of age and is buried in St Margaret's Churchyard, Stradishall. During the engagement on 12 August his fighter was hit and set on fire forcing a rapid belly-landing at Bembridge, on the Isle of Wight. He just managed to scramble clear before it exploded. His shared victory on 7 September followed a chase across the North Sea, shooting down the Dornier in flames over the Scheldt Estuary. He received a mention in despatches, gazetted on March 1941. His parents were Stuart F & Mrs Lillian E Williams of Johannesburg, South Africa, but originally from New Zealand.

Victories: 12 Aug   Ju88   Damaged
                18 Aug   Me109   Destroyed
                7 Sep   sh/Do17   Destroyed

Non-operational loss

?   Sgt E G Greenwood RAFVR
              245 Sqn
              Hurricane P3657

Based at Turnhouse, he dived into Loch Neagh and exploded, probably because of loss of oxygen. He was 22, son of Frank P and Mrs Florence H Greenwood of Leeds, Yorkshire. His body was not recovered so he has no known grave.

Tuesday, 22 October

15.30   F/O P C B St John RAF
              74 Sqn
              Spitfire P7431

Shot down by Me109, crashed at South Nutfield, Surrey. Saw action over Dunkirk, having arrived on 74 in April 1940. Buried in St Mary's Churchyard, Amersham, Bucks. Joined the RAF in September 1937; posted to 74 on 20 April 1940. Aged 23, he was the son of Robert H B & Mrs Edith Mary St John of Notting Hill, London.

Victories:	27 May	½ Do17	Destroyed
	10 Jul	Me 109	Probable
	10 Jul	Me109	Damaged
	28 Jul	Me109	Destroyed
	11 Sep	He111	Destroyed
	17 Oct	Me109	Destroyed

16.46   P/O N B Heywood RAF
              257 Sqn
              Hurricane R4195

Shot down over Folkestone by AA fire while in combat with Me109s, falling south of Lydd. Previously had been in France with 226 Squadron (Battles) and then with 32 and 607 Squadrons. Joined 257 on 14 October. He was 22 and was buried in Stretford Cemetery, Manchester. Joined the RAF in early 1939 and volunteered for fighters; had joined his first such squadron in September 1940.

16.50   Sgt R H B Fraser RAFVR
              257 Sqn
              Hurricane V6851

Shot down by Me109 over Folkestone. From Glasgow, he was one of the first pilots to join 257 when it reformed in May 1940. He was 20 years old and was buried in Craigton Cemetery, Glasgow. His parents were Adam & Mrs Mary F Fraser of Glasgow, Scotland. Joined the VR in July 1938. Posted to 257 on 17 May 1940.

16.50 Sgt J P Morrison RAFVR
46 Sqn
Hurricane R4074

Shot down in combat with fighters over Dungeness. Aged 25, he was buried in St Andrews & Jesmond Cemetery, Newcastle-upon-Tyne. Joined the VR in the summer of 1939, and his first squadron was No.17 which he went to on 31 August 1940. Moved to 46 on 17 September.

Wednesday, 23 October

No operational fatalities

Non-operational loss

10.55 P/O P R S Hurst RAF
600 Sqn
Blenheim L1272

Crashed into a hillside at Kirkby Malzeard, Yorkshire, flying in cloud, while engaged on a training flight. He came from Hampshire and was aged 20. Joining the RAF in October 1938 he had gone to 600 Squadron at Redhill in September 1940. Son of Eric & Mrs D A Hurst of Hannington, Hants, he is buried in Catterick Cemetery.

Thursday, 24 October

? P/O D T Jay DFC MiD RAF
87 Sqn
Hurricane P3404

Collided with another Hurricane returning from a patrol. Baled out but hit the tail-plane, knocking himself unconscious, so did not open his parachute and was killed. Born in London, he had previously been with No. 607 Squadron before moving to 87 in June 1940. Buried in Exeter High Cemetery, Heavitree, Exeter. He was 19, and the son of David S and Mrs Vera L Jay of Blackheath, SE London. Joined the RAF in March 1939. His DFC was gazetted on 22 October 1940.

Victories:	10 May	He111	Destroyed
	11 May	2/He111s	Destroyed
	11 May	½ He111	Destroyed

11 Jul	Me110	Destroyed
13 Aug	½Ju88	Destroyed
15 Aug	2/Ju87s	Destroyed
15 Aug	Me109	Destroyed
4/5 Sep	u/i ea	Damaged
15 Sep	½He111	Probable

Non-operational loss

17.20 P/O J Bury-Burzymski
303 Sqn
Hurricane V6807

Crashed during dog-fight practise. He had originally gone to 307 Squadron, moving to 303 on 11 October.

19.25 Sgt D R Stoodley RAFVR
43 Sqn
Hurricane V7303

Killed in a flying accident at Usworth. Had made six attempts to land cross-wind but finally he stalled at 250 feet and crashed. He hailed from Southampton and was aged 21. Had joined the VR in June 1939 and his posting to 43 Squadron came on 28 September 1940. Son of Harry & Mrs Adelaide E Stoodley, he is buried in the London Road Cemetery, Salisbury.

Friday, 25 October

? P/O S Piatkowski
79Sqn
Hurricane N2708

Crashed near Carew Cheriton, after routine patrol. Cause not known. Aged 28, from Poland, he is buried in St Illtyd's Churchyard, Pembrey, Carmarthenshire. He had been commissioned into the RAF in January 1940, and joined 79 Squadron on 11 September.

10.50 F/L F Jastrzebski
302 Sqn
Hurricane V7593

Missing from patrol over the Channel, last seen gliding towards France. Body washed ashore at Sylt and post war his remains were buried in Keil War Cemetery. Aged 34, he had been in the Polish military for some years before becoming a pilot.

CO of 132 Squadron of III/3 Fighter Dyon, seeing action over Poland and also with the French in May 1940. In July he joined the newly formed 302. He received the Virtuti Militari, the Cross of Valour & three bars, and the French Croix de Guerre.

Victories:	2 Sep '39	Ju86	Destroyed
	8 Sep '39	Me110	Destroyed
	10 Sep '39	Me109	Destroyed
	? May '40	EA	Destroyed
	? May	EA	½Destroyed
	15 Sep	½Do17	Destroyed
	18 Sep	Do17	Probable

12.07 P/O W B Pattullo RAF
46 Sqn
Hurricane V6804

Crashed in Romford, Essex, cause not known, during patrol. Severely injured and died the following day. Had earlier been with 151 and 249 Squadrons before moving to 46 in September. He was 21 and buried in St Andrew's Churchyard, North Weald Basset. He was the son of Patrick W & Mrs Jessie H B Pattulo of Eaglescliffe, Co. Durham.

Victories	30 Aug	Do17	Probable
	31 Aug	Do17	Destroyed
	11 Sep	½ He111	Destroyed
	15 Sep	Do17	Destroyed
	27 Sep	Me110	Destroyed
	27 Sep	½ Me109	Probable
	27 Sep	Ju88	Probable

15.25 P/O V Goth RAFVR
501 Sqn
Hurricane P2903

Collided with another Hurricane during combat with Me109s falling at Staplehurst, Kent. From Czechoslovakia he had earlier been with 310 Squadron until posted to 501 on 17 October. He was 25 and is buried at Sittingbourne & Milton Cemetery, Kent.

| Victories: | 7 Sep | Me110 | Destroyed |
| | 7 Sep | Me110 | Destroyed |

Non-operational loss

15.00   Sgt F Mills-Smith RAFVR
                601 Sqn
                Hurricane P3709

Collided with V6917 during a section training flight and crashed into the sea. No known grave.

15.00   Sgt L D May RAFVR
                601 Sqn
                Hurricane V6917

Collided with P3709 during a section training flight and crashed into the sea. No known grave.

Saturday, 26 October

11.30   F/O G M Simpson RAF
                229 Sqn
                Hurricane W6669

Shot down by Me109 while attacking He59 on the sea off the French coast. From New Zealand, born Christchurch 22 June 1919, he saw action over France and Dunkirk. He has no known grave and was the son of Herbert M & Mrs Hilda C Simpson. Joined the NZ territorials in February 1936, and when accepted by the RAF sailed for England in August 1938. Joined 229 in November 1939.

Victories:	18 May	He111	Damaged
	21 May	He111	Damaged
	21 May	Me110	Destroyed
	15 Sep	sh/He111	Destroyed
	15 Oct	Me109	Damaged

12.30   Sgt D W Elcome RAFVR
                602 Sqn
                Spitfire R6839

Failed to return from patrol. From Leigh-on-Sea, Essex, he was 21 years of age, and has no known grave. He was the son of Gilbert F & Mrs Isabel J Elcome of Leigh-on-Sea, Essex. Joined the VR in the summer of 1937, joining 602 on the 21 June 1940. He survived a crash on 10 September during a night-flying practice.

Victories:	31 Aug	Me109	Destroyed
	7 Sep	Me110	Destroyed

Non-operational loss

At this stage of the war and the Battle, it had become obvious that should the Germans switch to night bombing as winter approached, the RAF would be sorely tested, having few night fighter aircraft or trained pilots with knowledge of flying at night. Although the RAF had the Bristol Blenheims and the new Bristol Beaufighters were starting to arrive, it seemed expedient to use single seat fighters to help bridge the gap. The Hurricane was by far the better fighter to cope at night, but Spitfires were also used. Squadrons were starting to gain experience in night flying operations, and it caused a number of crashes, several of which were fatal.

20.40   Sgt D O Stanley RNZAF
            151 Sqn
            Hurricane V7434

Crashed taking off from Coleby Grange on night flying practice. Seriously injured, Stanley died the next day. He was 24, the son of William J & Mrs Annie Stanley of Auckland, New Zealand. He had learned to fly privately in 1938 and enrolled in the Civil Reserve of Pilots while training at Waikato Aero Club, Hamilton. Sailed to England in July 1940, joining 151 on 30 September. Buried in Scopwick Church Burial Ground, Lincolnshire.

20.55   Sgt R Holder RNZAF
            151 Sqn
            Hurricane R4185

Taking off from Coleby Grange on a night flying practice flight, stalled in a turn, crashed and was killed. He was 23, son of Charles & Mrs Kate Holder of Broom, Warwickshire. Buried in Bidford-on-Avon Burial Ground, Worcs. He was born at Bidford but went to New Zealand in 1938 to farm. Joined the RNZAF when war came and after training sailed for the UK in July. He was posted to 151 on 30 September. He had seen his fellow pilot crash shortly before and his flight commander asked if he would prefer not to fly, but he said he would be alright.

Sunday, 27 October

09.00   Sgt J A Scott RAFVR
74 Sqn
Spitfire P7526

Shot down by Me109 over Maidstone, crashing near Elmstead. He had previously had brief spells with 266 and 611 Squadrons. Son of John and Isabel Scott of Sudbury Hill, London. He was 22 and buried Alperton Burial Ground, Wembley, Middlesex. He had joined the VR in March 1939 and gone to 74 Squadron on 23 October 1940, being killed four days later.

14.05   F/O C W Goldsmith RAFVR
603 Sqn
Spitfire P7439

Shot down by Me109 south of Maidstone. Badly injured he died on the 28th. From Dersley, Transvaal, South Africa he was 23. With 603 and then briefly with 54 Squadron, he returned to 603 on 28 September. He is buried in Hornchurch Cemetery, Essex. His parents were Dr Arthur W & Mrs Nora V Goldsmith of Southbroom, Natal, South Africa. Educated in England at Cheltenham College and Imperial College, London, studying mines. Joined the University Air Squadron and then commissioned into the VR in March 1938.

14.05   P/O R B Dewey RAF
603 Sqn
Spitfire P7365

Shot down by Me109 of III/JG27 falling near Maidstone. From Portsmouth, he was with 611 Squadron until 27 September. Aged 19 he is buried in the Hornchurch Cemetery, Essex. He was the son of Alan & Mrs Violet Dewey. Joined the RAF in August 1939 and posted to 611 Squadron on 9 June 1940. Moved to 603 on 27 September.

Victories: 30 Sep   Me109   Destroyed
20 Oct   Me109   Destroyed

17.15   P/O A R I G Jottard
              145 Sqn
              Hurricane P3167

Shot down by Me109 south-east of the Isle of Wight. This 28-year-old Belgian Air Force pilot joined 145 on 17 August after escaping to England via Corsica, Casablanca and Gibraltar. This was accomplished in company with Jean Offenberg, having stolen two Caudron Simoun aircraft and flown them to Corsica. Arriving in England on 16 July 1940, he eventually arrived at 145 Squadron on 17 August. He has no known grave. His name appears on the Pelouse d'Honneur Cemetery memorial at Brussels, Evere.

Non-operational loss

08.30   P/O J R Mather RAFVR
              66 Sqn
              Spitfire P7539

Crashed and burned out at Half Moon Lane, Hildenborough, north-west of Tonbridge, Kent. Cause not known but probably oxygen loss. He was 25, son of Richard & Mrs M C L G A Mather of Ifield, Kent, and husband to Mrs Peggy Mather. Born in Blackheath, south-east London, he joined the RAFVR in June 1937 and was posted to 66 in April 1940. He was shot down in combat on 18 September but baled out without injury.

Victories: 10 Jul   sh/Do17   Destroyed
                 2 Sep   sh/He111   Destroyed

10.25   Sgt L V Toogood RAFVR
              43 Sqn
              Hurricane L1963

Engaged on high-altitude aerobatics, Toogood went into a vertical dive from 20,000 feet, possibly due to oxygen failure, and crashed fatally at Congburn Dean, Edmondsley, Durham. He was buried in Kingston Cemetery, Portsmouth. He had joined the VR in mid-1939, eventually being posted to No 43 Squadron on 28 September 1940. He was 20 years old.

Monday, 28 October

No operational fatalities

This was one of the rare days on which Fighter Command suffered no losses due to combat. However, the Germans lost four Me109s and a couple of bombers, with several other aircraft returning home with varying degrees of damage, both from air combat and anti-aircraft fire.

Tuesday, 29 October

Today saw the last great effort by the Luftwaffe, which mounted five raids. One headed for London and was engaged at around 11 am. The second, largely of fighter-bombers was also intercepted and a dozen of these raiders were shot down, many on the approaches to London. Three other raids, all by fighter-bombers (112 of them in all) made attacks on Portsmouth. Although ten RAF fighters were lost, only five pilots were killed. Some fourteen Me109s were lost, plus one Me110 and two Ju88s.

17.15   Sub-Lt A G Blake RN (pictured middle)
19 Sqn
Spitfire P7423

Missing from patrol, probably shot down by Me109 south of London. He crashed in Chelmsford. FAA pilot seconded to Fighter Command. From Slough, he was 23. He joined the Squadron on 1 July. Buried in Langley Marsh (St Mary's) Churchyard, Slough. Son of John H and Mrs Mary J Blake.

Victories:	3 Sep	Me109	Damaged
	9 Sep	He111	Destroyed
	15 Sep	Me109	Destroyed
	15 Sep	¼ He111	Destroyed
	15 Sep	Do17	Damaged
	17 Sep	Me109	Destroyed
	17 Sep	Me109	Destroyed

?   Sgt H E Black RAFVR
46 Sqn
Hurricane P3053

Shot down by Me109, crashed near Ashford. Born Measham, Leics, he was 26. Flew Battles in France with 226 Squadron, after which he became a volunteer for fighters, joining 32 Squadron on 3 September, then 257 on the 17th and finally to 46 in October. Badly burned he died in hospital on 9 November.

Buried in St Deny's Churchyard, Ibstock. Son of Herbert E & Mrs M E Black, husband to Gwen A Black of Ibstock, Leicestershire. Had joined the VR in the summer of 1937.

14.45   P/O R R Hutley RAFVR
                213 Sqn
                Hurricane V7622

Shot down off Selsey and baled out. Picked up by the Selsey lifeboat but he did not regain consciousness. He had been with 32 Squadron from 21 September, then 213 from 26 October. Buried in St Andrew's Churchyard, Tangmere aged 22. Joined the VR in late 1938.

L-R

P/O Landels P/O Sworder P/O Duncan P/O Thompson P/O Blackler P/O Hutley

P/O Goord P/O----- P/O Millard P/O MacMasters P/O Ross

**No 1 School of Army Co-Operation
RAF Old Sarum
August 1940**

15.10   P/O E Fechtner DFC RAF
                310 Sqn
                Hurricane P3889

Collided with another Hurricane during 'wing' patrol near Duxford. Aged 24, he is buried in Brookwood Military Cemetery. Born in Prague he served with the artillery until he transferred to the air force in 1937. Went to Poland and France, then finally to England and the RAF in July 1940.

Victories: 26 Aug   Me109   Destroyed
               31 Aug   Do17   Destroyed
               3 Sep   Me110   Destroyed
               7 Sep   Me110   Damaged
               18 Sep   Do17   Destroyed
               27 Sep   Do17   Probable

16.60   Sgt A G Girdwood RAFVR
                257 Sqn
                Hurricane V6852

Shot down by Me109 while taking off from North Weald, by Me109s from II(S)/LG2. Buried Hawkhead Cemetery, Paisley, Renfrewshire, aged 22. Son of Alexander & Mrs Margaret S Girdwood of Paisley. He joined the VR in the summer of 1938 and posted to 257 on 17 May 1940. After shooting down a Heinkel on 18 August he was himself shot down by a Me110 and wounded in the foot. He baled out over Foulness.

Victories: 13 Aug   Ju88   Destroyed
               18 Aug   sh/He111   Destroyed

Wednesday, 30 October

12.11   P/O A E Davies RAF
                222 Sqn
                Spitfire N3119

Shot down by Me109 and crashed near Crowhurst, Sussex. He had earlier been with 610 Squadron, moving to 222 on 28 September. He was 23 and buried in St Mary Magdalene Churchyard, Tamworth, Worcs. His parents were Alfred E & Mrs Norah Davies of Tamworth-in-Arden, and husband to Mrs Audrey M P Davies. A pre-war member of 604 Squadron AAF he was commissioned into the RAF in June 1939.

12.15 P/O H P M Edridge RAF
222 Sqn
Spitfire K9939

Shot down by Me109 and crashed trying to land at Ewhurst. He was taken from the wreckage but soon died of his injuries. He was 21 and buried in the Bath Roman Catholic Cemetery. Son of Ray and Mrs Georgina Edridge of Bath, Somerset. Joined the RAF in January 1939. Saw action over Dunkirk.

Victories:	1 Jun	Me109	Probable
	20 Oct	sh/Me110	Destroyed

13.00 P/O W H Millington DFC RAF
249 Sqn
Hurricane V7536

Missing from combat action over the Channel. Born in England, his family emigrated to Australia. Returning to join the RAF in June 1939, his first Squadron was No. 79 which he was posted to on 17 June 1940. He was then sent to 249 Squadron on 19 September. Has no known grave. He was 23 years old, son of William H & Mrs Elizabeth H Millington of Edwardstown, South Australia.

Victories:	9 Jul	Me109	Destroyed
	15 Aug	He111	Destroyed
	15 Aug	He111	Destroyed
	15 Aug	He111	Destroyed
	30 Aug	He111	Destroyed
	30 Aug	He111	Probable
	30 Aug	Me110	Damaged
	31 Aug	Do17	Destroyed
	31 Aug	Me109	Destroyed
	31 Aug	Me109	Probable
	27 Sep	Ju88	Destroyed
	27 Sep	½ Ju88	Destroyed
	7 Oct	Me109	Probable
	25 Oct	Me109	Probable
	28 Oct	Do17	Damaged
	28 Oct	¼ Ju88	Destroyed
	29 Oct	Me109	Probable

16.10   Sgt L A Garvey RAFVR
41 Sqn
Spitfire P7375

Shot down by Me109 over Ashford. From Birmingham, aged 26, he only joined the Squadron on the 10th. Buried in Witton Cemetery, in his home town. Son of Andrew J & Mrs Sarah A Garvey of Erdington, Birmingham. He was a well known athlete before the war, and joined the VR in June 1937. Joined 41 in October 1940.

20.10   P/O K W Worsdell RAF
Sgt E C Gardiner RAF
219 Sqn
Beaufighter R2065

Crashed returning from patrol in bad weather, after hitting trees. Born in Wakefield Worsdell, was 20 when he died, and buried in Nutfield Cemetery, Surrey. He was the son of Major Geoffrey B Worsdell (formerly of the Green Howards Yorkshire Regt) & Mrs Winifred M  Worsdell of Bracknell, Berkshire. He had been a Prize Cadet at the RAF College, Cranwell. Gardiner, from Pontefract, was 27 and is buried in his local cemetery. He was married to Freda Gardiner of Pontefract.

20.30   F/O H J Woodward DFC RAF
P/O A A Atkinson RAFVR
Sgt H T Perry RAFVR
23 Sqn
Blenheim L6721

Crashed near South Berstead, Sussex, following radio failure flying in bad weather conditions during night patrol. All three men died. Woodward, from  Heckmondwike, Yorkshire, was born in

Atkinson   *Perry*

Harefield, Middx. He had earlier been with 64 Squadron and had seen action over Dunkirk as a day fighter pilot and then during the Battle. Posted to 23 Squadron on 12 September. Buried in his local Yorkshire Cemetery. He was 24. His DFC was gazetted on 1 October 1940.

Atkinson was air gunner, aged 32, and buried in St Mary's Churchyard, Clymping, Sussex. Perry, radar operator, was from Saffron Walden, Essex, aged 23 and is buried in his local cemetery.

Woodward

Woodward's victories:

21 May	Me109	Damaged
31 May	Do17	Destroyed
19 Jul	Me109	by collision
5 Aug	Me109	Damaged
8 Aug	Me109	Destroyed
12 Aug	Me109	Destroyed
13 Aug	Do17	Destroyed

Thursday, 31 October

No operational fatalities

From this date German raids petered out as weather began to deteriorate. Although not totally appreciated at the time, 31 October is now generally accepted as the day the Battle of Britain came to an end. There would still be a number of small nuisance attacks during the following two months, mainly by bomb-carrying Me109 fighter-bombers, but the main effort against Britain came to an end.

List of Officially Accredited Battle of Britain Squadrons

This is a list of the officially accredited Battle of Britain units with their aircraft types, code letters, call signs and casualties.

On 9 November 1960 the Air Ministry published Air Ministry Order N850 which officially defined the qualifications for the classification of Battle of Britain Aircrew. The AMO also stated the Squadrons which were deemed to have fought in the Battle under the control of RAF Fighter Command between 0001 hours on 10 July and 2359 hours on 31 October 1940; the official beginning and end of the Battle.

A total of 71 Squadrons and other units from Fighter Command, Coastal Command and the Fleet Air Arm are listed.[1]

Squadron	Squadron Code	Radio call sign	Aircraft Type	Number of Casualties
No. 1 (Cawnpore) Squadron RAF	JX	ACORN	Hurricane	7
No. 3 Squadron RAF	OQ		Hurricane	1
No. 17 Squadron RAF	YB	EDEY	Hurricane	5
No. 19 Squadron RAF	QV	LUTON	Spitfire	6
No. 23 Squadron RAF	YP	LUTON	Blenheim	8
No. 25 Squadron RAF	ZK	LUTON	Blenheim, Beaufighter	5
No. 29 Squadron RAF	RO		Blenheim	8
No. 32 Squadron RAF	GZ	JACKO	Hurricane	2
No. 41 Squadron RAF	EB	MITOR	Spitfire	11[2]
No. 43 (China-British) Squadron RAF	FT		Hurricane	14
No. 46 (Uganda) Squadron RAF	PO	ANGEL	Hurricane	14
No. 54 Squadron RAF	KL	RABBIT	Spitfire	6
No. 56 (Punjab) Squadron RAF	US	BAFFIN	Hurricane	8
No. 64 Squadron RAF	SH	FREEMA	Spitfire	7
No. 65 (East India) Squadron RAF	YT		Spitfire	8

The Fallen Few of the Battle of Britain

Squadron	Squadron Code	Radio call sign	Aircraft Type	Number of Casualties
No. 66 Squadron RAF	LZ	FIBIUS	Spitfire	8
No. 72 (Basutoland) Squadron RAF	RN	TENNIS	Spitfire	9
No. 73 Squadron RAF	TP		Hurricane	4
No. 74 Squadron RAF	ZP	DYSOE	Spitfire	12
No. 79 (Madras Presidency) Squadron RAF	NV	PANSY	Hurricane	4
No. 85 Squadron RAF	VY	HYDRO	Hurricane	7
No. 87 (United Provinces) Squadron RAF	LK	SUNCUP	Hurricane	7
No. 92 (East India) Squadron RAF	QJ	GANNIC	Spitfire	14
No. 111 Squadron RAF	JU	WAGON	Hurricane	11
No. 141 Squadron RAF	TW		Boulton Paul Defiant	10
No. 145 Squadron RAF	SO	PATIN	Hurricane	13
No. 151 Squadron RAF	DZ		Hurricane	11
No. 152 (Hyderabad) Squadron RAF	UM	MAIDA	Spitfire	14
No. 213 (Ceylon) Squadron RAF	AK	BEARSKIN	Hurricane	15
No. 219 (Mysore) Squadron RAF	FK		Blenheim, Beaufighter	6
No. 222 (Natal) Squadron RAF	ZD	KOTEL	Spitfire	9
No. 229 Squadron RAF	RE	KETA	Hurricane	5
No. 232 Squadron RAF	EF		Hurricane	-
No. 234 (Madras Presidency) Squadron RAF	AZ	CRESSY	Spitfire	5
No. 238 Squadron RAF	VK		Hurricane	17

List of Officially Accredited Battle of Britain Squadrons

Squadron	Squadron Code	Radio call sign	Aircraft Type	Number of Casualties
No. 242 (Canadian) Squadron RAF	LE	LORAG	Hurricane	5
No. 245 (Northern Rhodesia) Squadron RAF	DX		Hurricane	2
No. 247 (China - British) Squadron RAF	HP		Gloster Gladiator	-
No. 249 (Gold Coast) Squadron RAF	GN	GANER	Hurricane	8
No. 253 (Hyderabad) Squadron RAF	SW	VICEROY	Hurricane	11
No. 257 (Burma) Squadron RAF	DT	ALERT	Hurricane	11
No. 263 (Fellowship of the Bellows) Squadron RAF	HE		Hurricane, Westland Whirlwind	1
No. 264 (Madras Presidency) Squadron RAF	PS		Boulton Paul Defiant	18
No. 266 (Rhodesia) Squadron RAF	UO		Spitfire	7
No. 421 Flight RAF	L-Z		Hurricane, Spitfire	1
No. 422 Flight RAF	-		Hurricane	-
Fighter Interception Unit	-		Hurricane, Blenheim, Beaufighter	-
Auxiliary Squadrons				
No. 501 (County of Gloucester) Squadron AuxAF	SD	MANDREL	Hurricane	19
No. 504 (City of Nottingham) Squadron AuxAF	TM		Hurricane	6
No. 600 (City of London) Squadron AuxAF	BQ		Blenheim, Beaufighter	9

The Fallen Few of the Battle of Britain

Squadron	Squadron Code	Radio call sign	Aircraft Type	Number of Casualties
No. 601 (County of London) Squadron AuxAF	UF	WEAPON	Hurricane	14
No. 602 (City of Glasgow) Squadron AuxAF	LO	VILLA	Spitfire	5
No. 603 (City of Edinburgh) Squadron AuxAF	XT	VIKEN	Spitfire	13
No. 604 (County of Middlesex) Squadron AuxAF	NG	TALLYHO	Blenheim, Beaufighter	3
No. 605 (County of Warwick) Squadron AuxAF	UP	TURKEY	Hurricane	8
No. 607 (County of Durham) Squadron AuxAF	AF		Hurricane	9
No. 609 (West Riding) Squadron AuxAF	PR	SORBO	Spitfire	7
No. 610 (County of Chester) Squadron AuxAF	DW	DOGROSE	Spitfire	11
No. 611 (West Lancashire) Squadron AuxAF	FY	CHARLIE	Spitfire	2
No. 615 (County of Surrey) Squadron AuxAF	KW	PANTA	Hurricane	6
No. 616 (South Yorkshire) Squadron AuxAF	QJ[3]	RADPOE	Spitfire	6

Commonwealth and Allied squadrons

No. 1 Squadron RCAF (Canadian)	YO	CARIBOU	Hurricane	3
302 (City of Poznan) Squadron (Polish)[4]	WX	CALEB	Hurricane	6

List of Officially Accredited Battle of Britain Squadrons

Squadron	Squadron Code	Radio call sign	Aircraft Type	Number of Casualties
303 (Warsaw - Kosciuszko) Squadron (Polish)[5]	RF	APANY	Hurricane	7
No. 310 (Czechoslovak) Squadron (Czech)	NN	CALLA	Hurricane	4
No. 312 (Czechoslovak) Squadron (Czech)	DU	SILVO	Hurricane	1
Coastal Command Squadrons				
No. 235 Squadron RAF	QY		Blenheim	14
No. 236 Squadron RAF	FA		Blenheim	10
No. 248 Squadron RAF	WR		Blenheim	16
Fleet Air Arm (FAA) Squadrons				
No. 804 Squadron FAA	5-		Gloster Sea Gladiator / Grumman Martlet	-
No. 808 Squadron FAA	5-		Fairey Fulmar[6]	-

Notes

1. Ramsay, 1989, pp.252–255.
2. 41 Squadron's Battle of Britain pilots comprised 49 men aged from 18 to 32. Forty-two were British, three Irish, two Canadian and two New Zealanders. Casualties were sustained by almost half the men: eleven (22.5 per cent) were killed and twelve (24.5 per cent) were wounded, and one of the Squadron's ground crew was killed in the Blitz.
3. Note: The squadron code letters QJ were the same as those of 92 Squadron. The codes changed to YQ in 1941.
4. *Poznański*.
5. *Warszawski im. Tadeusza Kościuszki*.
6. In normal naval use flown with a navigator, these were flown solo.

Index

Index

Gamblen, F/O D. R., RAF, 19

Gane, P/O S. R., RAF, 163

Gardiner, Sgt E. C., RAF, 177

Gardner, P/O J. R., RAF, 10

Garfield, Sgt W. J., RAFVR, 108–109

Garvey, Sgt L. S., RAFVR, 177

Garvin, S/L G. D., RAF, 69

Gaskell, P/O R. S., RAF, 60

Gaunt, P/O G. N., AAF, 112

Gillan, F/O J., RAF, 32

Gillies, F/L K. McL., RAF, 144

Gillman, P/O K. R., RAF, 63

Girdwood, Sgt A. G., RAFVR, 175

Gledhill, Sgt G., RAFVR, 30

Glowacki, P/O W. J., PAF, 121–2

Glyde, F/O R. L., DFC RAF, 40–1

Gmur, Sgt F., RAF, 72

Goldsmith, F/O C. W., RAFVR, 171

Goodall, P/O H. I., RAFVR, 150

Goodwin, F/O H, MacD., AAF, 43

Goodwin, Sgt C., RAFVR, 139

Gordon, P/O W. H. G., RAF, 92

Gore, F/L W. E., DFC AAF, 135

Goth, P/O V., RAFVR, 168

Gouldstone, Sgt R. J., AAF, 64

Gray, Sgt M., RAFVR, 89

Green, P/O A. W. V., RAFVR, 107

Green, P/O M. D., RAFVR, 163

Greenshields, Sub-Lt H. LaF., RNVR, 48

Greenwood, Sgt E. G., RAFVR, 164–5

Gregory, P/O F. S., RAF, 42

Grice, F/O D. N., RAFVR, 25–6

Gruszka, F/O F., PAF, 53

Gunning, P/O P. S., RAF, 159

Gunter, P/O E. M., RAFVR, 129

Gurteen, P/O J. V., RAFVR, 113

Guy, Sgt L. N., RAFVR, 54

Haigh, Sgt C., RAF, 65

Hall, F/L N. M., AFC RAF, 26

Halton, Sgt D. W., RAFVR, 44

Hamar, P/O J. R., DFC RAFO, 14

Hamilton, F/L H. R., RAF, 71

Hamilton, P/O A. C., RAF, 9

Hanson, F/O D. H. W., RAF, 82–3

Hanzlicek, Sgt O., CAF, 154

Hardacre, F/O J. R., RAF, 138

Hargreaves, P/O F. N., RAF, 105

Harrison, P/O D. S., RAFVR, 134

Harrison, P/O J. H., RAFVR, 38

Harrold, P/O F. C., RAF, 132

Hastings, P/O D., RAF, 150

Hawkings, Sgt R. P., RAFVR, 54

Hawley, Sgt F. B., RAFVR, 45

Haworth, F/O J. F. J., RAF, 12

Head, Sgt F. A. P., RAFVR, 22

Head, Sgt G. M., RAF, 156

Helcke, Sgt D. A., RAFVR, 116–17

Hewitt, P/O D. A., RAFVR, 4

Heywood, P/O N. B., RAF, 165

Higgins, Sgt W. B., RAFVR, 110

Higgs, F/O T. P. K., RAF, 2

Hight, P/O C. H., RAF, 46

Hill, P/O H. P., RAF, 119

Hillcoat, F/L H. B. L., AAF, 84

Hlavac, Sgt J., CAF, 153

Hobson, P/O C. A., RAF, 143

Hogg, P/O D. W., RAFVR, 83

Hogg, P/O R. M., RAF, 60

Holder, Sgt R., RNZAF, 170

Holland, P/O D. F., RAFVR, 118

Holland, Sgt K. C., RAFVR, 122

Homer, F/O M. G., DFC RAF, 129

Hood, S/L H. R. L., RAF, 90

Hope, F/O R., RAF, 157

Horsky, Sgt V., CAF, 124

Houghton, Sgt O. V., RAFVR, 91

Howes, P/O P., RAFVR, 117

Howley, P/O R. A., RAF, 9

Hughes, F/L D. P., RAF, 105

Hughes, F/L P. C., DFC RAF, 99

Hughes, Sgt D. E., RNZAF, 143

Hull, S/L C. B., DFC RAF, 11, 94

Hunter, S/L P. A., DSO RAF, 59

Hurst, P/O P. R. S., RAF, 166

Hutley, P/O R. R., RAFVR, 174

Ireland, Sgt S., RAFVR, 4

Irving, F/L M. M., AAF, 135

Isaac, Sgt L. R., RAFVR, 23

Jacobson, AC2 N., RAFVR, 64

Jackson, AC2 A., RAF, 157

Neville, Sgt W. J., RAFVR, 35
Noble, Sgt D., RAFVR, 71
Nokes-Cooper, F/O B., RAFVR, 22
Norris, Sgt P. P., RAFVR, 41

O'Brien, S/L J. S., DFC RAF, 98
O'Malley, F/O D. K. C., RAFVR, 87
O'Neill, F/O D. H., RAF, 155
Oelofse, P/O J. R. S., RAF, 28
Oldfield, Sgt T. G., AAF, 130
Orgias, P/O E., RAF, 123
Ostowicz, F/O A., KW RAF, 30

Pankratz, F/L W., RAF, 39
Parker, Sgt K. B., RAFVR, 158
Parkinson, Sgt C., RAFVR, 11
Parnell, P/O S. B., AAF, 101
Paszkiewicz, F/O L. W., PAF, 125
Paterson, F/L J. A., RAF, 125
Patterson, Mid. P. J., FAA, 57
Patterson, P/O R. L., RAFVR, 7
Pattinson, F/O A. J. S., RAF, 156
Pattison, Sgt K. C., RAFVR, 155
Pattullo, P/O W. B., RAF, 168
Paul, Sub-Lt F. D., FAA, 16
Payne, AC2 R. I., RAFVR, 123
Peacock, Sgt W. A., AAF, 104
Pearson, Sgt G. W., RAFVR, 91–2
Pease, F/O A. P., RAFVR, 113
Peel, F/O C. D., AAF, 7
Perry, Sgt H.T., RAFVR, 177
Peters, F/O G. C. B., RAF, 136
Peterson, F/O O. J., RCAF, 124
Philippart, P/O J. A. L., RAFVR, 61
Phillips, F/Sgt N. T., RAF, 25
Piatkowski, P/O S., RAF, 167
Pidd, Sgt L., RAFVR, 113
Pigg, F/O O. StJ., RAF, 78
Pinkham, S/L P. C., AFC RAF, 88
Plummer, F/O R. P., RAF, 86
Ponting, P/O W. A., RAF, 59
Posener, P/O F. H., RAF, 12
Pyman, P/O L. L., RAFVR, 51

Ramsay, P/O J. B., RAF, 54
Ramshaw, Sgt J. W., RAFVR, 86

Rasmussen, Sgt L. A. W., RNZAF, 87
Ravenhill, F/O M., RAF, 137–8
Reddington, Sgt L. A. E., RAFVR, 138
Reilley, P/O H. W., RAF, 160
Reynell, F/L R. C., RAFO, 95
Rhodes, P/O R. A., RAF, 64
Rhodes-Moorhouse, F.L W. H., DFC AAF, 32, 93
Ricalton, F/O A. L., RAF, 160
Ridley, Sgt M., RAF, 65
Rigby, P/O R. H., RAF, 8
Rimmer, F/L R. F., RAF, 131
Ringwood, Sgt E. A., RAF, 67
Ritchie, Sgt R. D., RAFVR, 29
Rose-Price, F/O A. T., RAF, 82
Round, Sgt J. H., RAFVR, 56
Rozwadowski, P/O M., RAF, 47
Rushmer, F/L F. W., AAF, 88

Samolinski, P/O W. M. C., RAF, 123
Sanders, F/O D. J., RAF, 100
Saunders, Sgt A. F. C., RAFVR, 99
Sawyer, S/L H. C., RAF, 23
Schwind, F/L L. H., RAF, 125
Sclanders, P/O K. M., RAFVR, 102
Scott, F/O W. J. M., RAFVR, 100
Scott, Sgt E., RAF, 131
Scott, Sgt J. A., RAFVR, 171
Sears, P/O L. A., RAF, 24
Sharp, Sgt B. R., RAFVR, 107
Shaw, F/O I. G., RAF, 59
Shaw, P/O R. H., RAFVR, 83
Shepherd, Sgt F. E. R., AAF, 104
Shepley, P/O D. C., RAF, 38
Shepperd, Sgt E. E., RAF, 161
Shepperd, Sgt G. E., RAF, 139
Shorrocks, P/O N. B., RAFVR, 107
Sibley, Sgt F. A., RAFVR, 142
Silver, Sgt W. G., RAF, 122
Sim, Sgt R. B., RAFVR, 37
Simpson, F/O G. M., 169,
Siudak, Sgt A., PAF, 145
Slatter, P/O D. M., RAF, 10
Sly, Sgt O. K., RAFVR, 157
Smith, F/O D. S., RAF, 128
Smith, P/O D. N. E., RAFVR, 35

Index